W9-AVC-914

Multiplication and Division

Packages and Groups

Grade 4

Also appropriate for Grade 5

Karen Economopoulos
Susan Jo Russell
Cornelia Tierney

Developed at TERC, Cambridge, Massachusetts

Dale Seymour Publications®
Menlo Park, California

The *Investigations* curriculum was developed at TERC (formerly
Technical Education Research Centers) in collaboration with Kent State
University and the State University of New York at Buffalo. The work was
supported in part by National Science Foundation Grant No. ESI-9050210.
TERC is a nonprofit company working to improve mathematics and science
education. TERC is located at 2067 Massachusetts Avenue, Cambridge,
MA 02140.

This project was supported, in part,
by the
National Science Foundation
Opinions expressed are those of the authors
and not necessarily those of the Foundation

Managing Editor: Catherine Anderson
Series Editor: Beverly Cory
Revision Team: Laura Marshall Alavosus, Ellen Harding, Patty Green Holubar,
Suzanne Knott, Beverly Hersh Lozoff
ESL Consultant: Nancy Sokol Green
Production/Manufacturing Director: Janet Yearian
Production/Manufacturing Coordinator: Joe Conte
Design Manager: Jeff Kelly
Design: Don Taka
Illustrations: Barbara Epstein-Eagle, Hollis Burkhart
Cover: Bay Graphics
Composition: Archetype Book Composition

This book is published by Dale Seymour Publications®, an imprint of
Addison Wesley Longman, Inc.

Dale Seymour Publications
2725 Sand Hill Road
Menlo Park, CA 94025
Customer Service: 800-872-1100

Order number DS43898
ISBN 1-57232-751-0

4 5 6 7 8 9 10-ML-01 00 99

Printed on Recycled Paper

TERC

INVESTIGATIONS IN NUMBER, DATA, AND SPACE®

Principal Investigator   Susan Jo Russell

Co-Principal Investigator   Cornelia C. Tierney

Director of Research and Evaluation   Jan Mokros

Curriculum Development
Joan Akers
Michael T. Battista
Mary Berle-Carman
Douglas H. Clements
Karen Economopoulos
Ricardo Nemirovsky
Andee Rubin
Susan Jo Russell
Cornelia C. Tierney
Amy Shulman Weinberg

Evaluation and Assessment
Mary Berle-Carman
Abouali Farmanfarmaian
Jan Mokros
Mark Ogonowski
Amy Shulman Weinberg
Tracey Wright
Lisa Yaffee

Teacher Support
Rebecca B. Corwin
Karen Economopoulos
Tracey Wright
Lisa Yaffee

Technology Development
Michael T. Battista
Douglas H. Clements
Julie Sarama Meredith
Andee Rubin

Video Production
David A. Smith

Administration and Production
Amy Catlin
Amy Taber

*Cooperating Classrooms
for This Unit*
Michele de Silva
Jim Samson
Boston Public Schools
Boston, MA

Kathleen D. O'Connell
Linda Verity
Arlington Public Schools
Arlington, MA

Consultants and Advisors
Elizabeth Badger
Deborah Lowenberg Ball
Marilyn Burns
Ann Grady
Joanne M. Gurry
James J. Kaput
Steven Leinwand
Mary M. Lindquist
David S. Moore
John Olive
Leslie P. Steffe
Peter Sullivan
Grayson Wheatley
Virginia Woolley
Anne Zarinnia

Graduate Assistants
Kent State University
Joanne Caniglia
Pam DeLong
Carol King

State University of New York at Buffalo
Rosa Gonzalez
Sue McMillen
Julie Sarama Meredith
Sudha Swaminathan

Revisions and Home Materials
Cathy Miles Grant
Marlene Kliman
Margaret McGaffigan
Megan Murray
Kim O'Neil
Andee Rubin
Susan Jo Russell
Lisa Seyferth
Myriam Steinback
Judy Storeygard
Anna Suarez
Cornelia Tierney
Carol Walker
Tracey Wright

CONTENTS

WHERE TO START

The first-time user of *Packages and Groups* should read the following:

When you next teach this same unit, you can begin to read more of the background. Each time you present the unit, you will learn more about how your students understand the mathematical ideas.

Investigations in Number, Data, and Space® is a K–5 mathematics curriculum with four major goals:

- to offer students meaningful mathematical problems
- to emphasize depth in mathematical thinking rather than superficial exposure to a series of fragmented topics
- to communicate mathematics content and pedagogy to teachers
- to substantially expand the pool of mathematically literate students

The *Investigations* curriculum embodies a new approach based on years of research about how children learn mathematics. Each grade level consists of a set of separate units, each offering 2–8 weeks of work. These units of study are presented through investigations that involve students in the exploration of major mathematical ideas.

Approaching the mathematics content through investigations helps students develop flexibility and confidence in approaching problems, fluency in using mathematical skills and tools to solve problems, and proficiency in evaluating their solutions. Students also build a repertoire of ways to communicate about their mathematical thinking, while their enjoyment and appreciation of mathematics grows.

The investigations are carefully designed to invite all students into mathematics—girls and boys, members of diverse cultural, ethnic, and language groups, and students with different strengths and interests. Problem contexts often call on students to share experiences from their family, culture, or community. The curriculum eliminates barriers—such as work in isolation from peers, or emphasis on speed and memorization—that exclude some students from participating successfully in mathematics. The following aspects of the curriculum ensure that all students are included in significant mathematics learning:

- Students spend time exploring problems in depth.
- They find more than one solution to many of the problems they work on.
- They invent their own strategies and approaches, rather than relying on memorized procedures.
- They choose from a variety of concrete materials and appropriate technology, including calculators, as a natural part of their everyday mathematical work.
- They express their mathematical thinking through drawing, writing, and talking.
- They work in a variety of groupings—as a whole class, individually, in pairs, and in small groups.
- They move around the classroom as they explore the mathematics in their environment and talk with their peers.

While reading and other language activities are typically given a great deal of time and emphasis in elementary classrooms, mathematics often does not get the time it needs. If students are to experience mathematics in depth, they must have enough time to become engaged in real mathematical problems. We believe that a minimum of five hours of mathematics classroom time a week—about an hour a day—is critical at the elementary level. The plan and pacing of the *Investigations* curriculum is based on that belief.

We explain more about the pedagogy and principles that underlie these investigations in Teacher Notes throughout the units. For correlations of the curriculum to the NCTM Standards and further help in using this research-based program for teaching mathematics, see the following books:

- *Implementing the* Investigations in Number, Data, and Space® *Curriculum*

- *Beyond Arithmetic: Changing Mathematics in the Elementary Classroom* by Jan Mokros, Susan Jo Russell, and Karen Economopoulos

This book is one of the curriculum units for *Investigations in Number, Data, and Space.* In addition to providing part of a complete mathematics curriculum for your students, this unit offers information to support your own professional development. You, the teacher, are the person who will make this curriculum come alive in the classroom; the book for each unit is your main support system.

Although the curriculum does not include student textbooks, reproducible sheets for student work are provided in the unit and are also available as Student Activity Booklets. Students work actively with objects and experiences in their own environment and with a variety of manipulative materials and technology, rather than with a book of instruction and problems. We strongly recommend use of the overhead projector as a way to present problems, to focus group discussion, and to help students share ideas and strategies.

Ultimately, every teacher will use these investigations in ways that make sense for his or her particular style, the particular group of students, and the constraints and supports of a particular school environment. Each unit offers information and guidance for a wide variety of situations, drawn from our collaborations with many teachers and students over many years. Our goal in this book is to help you, a professional educator, implement this curriculum in a way that will give all your students access to mathematical power.

Investigation Format

The opening two pages of each investigation help you get ready for the work that follows.

What Happens This gives a synopsis of each session or block of sessions.

Mathematical Emphasis This lists the most important ideas and processes students will encounter in this investigation.

What to Plan Ahead of Time These lists alert you to materials to gather, sheets to duplicate, transparencies to make, and anything else you need to do before starting.

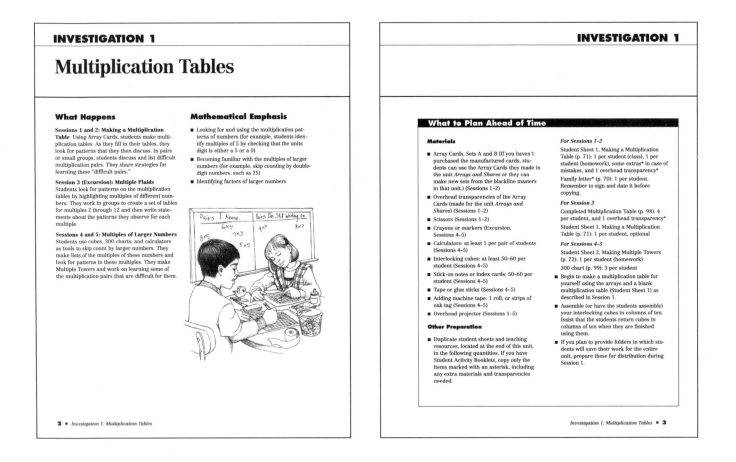

INVESTIGATION 1

Multiplication Tables

What Happens

Sessions 1 and 2: Making a Multiplication Table Using Array Cards, students make multiplication tables. As they fill in their tables, they look for patterns that they then discuss. In pairs or small groups, students discuss and list difficult multiplication pairs. They share strategies for learning these "difficult pairs."

Session 3 (Excursion): Multiple Plaids Students look for patterns on the multiplication tables by highlighting multiples of different numbers. They work in groups to create a set of tables for multiples 2 through 12 and then write statements about the patterns they observe for each multiple.

Sessions 4 and 5: Multiples of Larger Numbers Students use cubes, 300 charts, and calculators as tools to skip count by larger numbers. They make lists of the multiples of these numbers and look for patterns in these multiples. They make Multiple Towers and work on learning some of the multiplication pairs that are difficult for them.

Mathematical Emphasis

■ Looking for and using the multiplication patterns of numbers (for example, students identify multiples of 5 by checking that the units digit is either a 5 or a 0)

■ Becoming familiar with the multiples of larger numbers (for example, skip counting by double-digit numbers, such as 25)

■ Identifying factors of larger numbers

What to Plan Ahead of Time

Materials

■ Array Cards, Sets A and B (If you haven't purchased the manufactured cards, students can use the Array Cards they made in the unit *Arrays and Shares* or they can make new sets from the blackline masters in that unit.) (Sessions 1–2)

■ Overhead transparencies of the Array Cards (made for the unit *Arrays and Shares*) (Sessions 1–2)

■ Scissors (Sessions 1–2)

■ Crayons or markers (Excursion, Sessions 4–5)

■ Calculators: at least 1 per pair of students (Sessions 4–5)

■ Interlocking cubes: at least 50–60 per student (Sessions 4–5)

■ Stick-on notes or index cards: 50–60 per student (Sessions 4–5)

■ Tape or glue sticks (Sessions 4–5)

■ Adding machine tape: 1 roll; or strips of oak tag (Sessions 4–5)

■ Overhead projector (Sessions 1–5)

Other Preparation

■ Duplicate student sheets and teaching resources, located at the end of this unit, in the following quantities. If you have Student Activity Booklets, copy only the items marked with an asterisk, including any extra materials and transparencies needed.

For Sessions 1–2
Student Sheet 1, Making a Multiplication Table (p. 71): 1 per student (class), 1 per student (homework), some extras* in case of mistakes, and 1 overhead transparency*
Family letter* (p. 70): 1 per student. Remember to sign and date it before copying.

For Session 3
Completed Multiplication Table (p. 98): 4 per student, and 1 overhead transparency*
Student Sheet 1, Making a Multiplication Table (p. 71): 1 per student, optional

For Sessions 4–5
Student Sheet 2, Making Multiple Towers (p. 72): 1 per student (homework)
300 chart (p. 99): 3 per student

■ Begin to make a multiplication table for yourself using the arrays and a blank multiplication table (Student Sheet 1) as described in Session 1.

■ Assemble (or have the students assemble) your interlocking cubes in columns of ten. Insist that the students return cubes in columns of ten when they are finished using them.

■ If you plan to provide folders in which students will save their work for the entire unit, prepare these for distribution during Session 1.

Sessions Within an investigation, the activities are organized by class session, a session being at least a one-hour math class. Sessions are numbered consecutively through an investigation. Often several sessions are grouped together, presenting a block of activities with a single major focus.

When you find a block of sessions presented together—for example, Sessions 1, 2, and 3—read through the entire block first to understand the overall flow and sequence of the activities. Make some preliminary decisions about how you will divide the activities into three sessions for your class, based on what you know about your students. You may need to modify your initial plans as you progress through the activities, and you may want to make notes in the margins of the pages as reminders for the next time you use the unit.

Be sure to read the Session Follow-Up section at the end of the session block to see what homework assignments and extensions are suggested as you make your initial plans.

While you may be used to a curriculum that tells you exactly what each class session should cover, we have found that the teacher is in a better position to make these decisions. Each unit is flexible and may be handled somewhat differently by every teacher. While we provide guidance for how many sessions a particular group of activities is likely to need, we want you to be active in determining an appropriate pace and the best transition points for your class. It is not unusual for a teacher to spend more or less time than is proposed for the activities.

Ten-Minute Math At the beginning of some sessions, you will find Ten-Minute Math activities. These are designed to be used in tandem with the investigations, but not during the math hour. Rather, we hope you will do them whenever you have a spare 10 minutes—maybe before lunch or recess, or at the end of the day.

Ten-Minute Math offers practice in key concepts, but not always those being covered in the unit. For example, in a unit on using data, Ten-Minute Math might revisit geometric activities done earlier in the year. Complete directions for the suggested activities are included at the end of each unit.

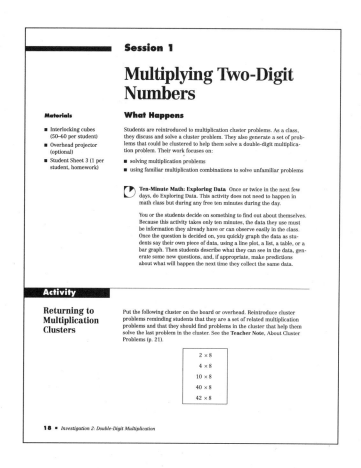

Activities The activities include pair and small-group work, individual tasks, and whole-class discussions. In any case, students are seated together, talking and sharing ideas during all work times. Students most often work cooperatively, although each student may record work individually.

Choice Time In some units, some sessions are structured with activity choices. In these cases, students may work simultaneously on different activities focused on the same mathematical ideas. Students choose which activities they want to do, and they cycle through them.

You will need to decide how to set up and introduce these activities and how to let students make their choices. Some teachers present them as station activities, in different parts of the room. Some list the choices on the board as reminders or have students keep their own lists.

Extensions Sometimes in Session Follow-Up, you will find suggested extension activities. These are opportunities for some or all students to explore a topic in greater depth or in a different context. They are not designed for "fast" students; mathematics is a multifaceted discipline, and different students will want to go further in different investigations. Look for and encourage the sparks of interest and enthusiasm you see in your students, and use the extensions to help them pursue these interests.

Excursions Some of the *Investigations* units include excursions—blocks of activities that could be omitted without harming the integrity of the unit. This is one way of dealing with the great depth and variety of elementary mathematics—much more than a class has time to explore in any one year. Excursions give you the flexibility to make different choices from year to year, doing the excursion in one unit this time, and next year trying another excursion.

Tips for the Linguistically Diverse Classroom At strategic points in each unit, you will find concrete suggestions for simple modifications of the teaching strategies to encourage the participation of all students. Many of these tips offer alternative ways to elicit critical thinking from students at varying levels of English proficiency, as well as from other students who find it difficult to verbalize their thinking.

The tips are supported by suggestions for specific vocabulary work to help ensure that all students can participate fully in the investigations. The Preview for the Linguistically Diverse Classroom (p. I-19) lists important words that are assumed as part of the working vocabulary of the unit. Second-language learners will need to become familiar with these words in order to understand the problems and activities they will be doing. These terms can be incorporated into students' second-language work before or during the unit. Activities that can be used to present the words are found in the appendix, Vocabulary Support for Second-Language Learners (p. 67). In addition, ideas for making connections to students' language and cultures, included on the Preview page, help the class explore the unit's concepts from a multicultural perspective.

Materials

A complete list of the materials needed for teaching this unit is found on p. I-16. Some of these materials are available in kits for the *Investigations* curriculum. Individual items can also be purchased from school supply dealers.

Classroom Materials In an active mathematics classroom, certain basic materials should be available at all times: interlocking cubes, pencils, unlined paper, graph paper, calculators, things to count with, and measuring tools. Some activities in this curriculum require scissors and glue sticks or tape. Stick-on notes and large paper are also useful materials throughout.

So that students can independently get what they need at any time, they should know where these materials are kept, how they are stored, and how they are to be returned to the storage area. For example, interlocking cubes are best stored in towers of ten; then, whatever the activity, they should be returned to storage in groups of ten at the end of the hour. You'll find that establishing such routines at the beginning of the year is well worth the time and effort.

Technology Calculators are used throughout *Investigations.* Many of the units recommend that you have at least one calculator for each pair. You will find calculator activities, plus Teacher Notes discussing this important mathematical tool, in an early unit at each grade level. It is assumed that calculators will be readily available for student use.

Computer activities at grade 4 use a software program that was developed especially for the *Investigations* curriculum. The program *Geo-Logo*™ is used for activities in the 2-D Geometry unit, *Sunken Ships and Grid Patterns,* where students explore coordinate graphing systems, the use of negative numbers to represent locations in space, and the properties of geometric figures.

How you use the computer activities depends on the number of computers you have available. Suggestions are offered in the geometry units for how to organize different types of computer environments.

Children's Literature Each unit offers a list of suggested children's literature (p. I-16) that can be used to support the mathematical ideas in the unit. Sometimes an activity is based on a specific children's book, with suggestions for substitutions where practical. While such activities can be adapted and taught without the book, the literature offers a rich introduction and should be used whenever possible.

Student Sheets and Teaching Resources Student recording sheets and other teaching tools needed for both class and homework are provided as reproducible blackline masters at the end of each unit. They are also available as Student Activity Booklets. These booklets contain all the sheets each student will need for individual work, freeing you from extensive copying (although you may need or want to copy the occasional teaching resource on transparency film or card stock, or make extra copies of a student sheet).

We think it's important that students find their own ways of organizing and recording their work. They need to learn how to explain their thinking with both drawings and written words, and how to organize their results so someone else can under-

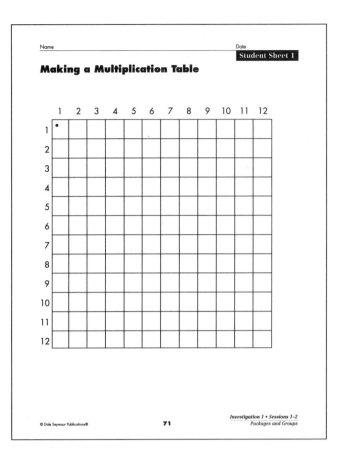

stand them. For this reason, we deliberately do not provide student sheets for every activity. Regardless of the form in which students do their work, we recommend that they keep a mathematics notebook or folder so that their work is always available for reference.

Homework In *Investigations,* homework is an extension of classroom work. Sometimes it offers review and practice of work done in class, sometimes preparation for upcoming activities, and sometimes numerical practice that revisits work in earlier units. Homework plays a role both in supporting students' learning and in helping inform families about the ways in which students in this curriculum work with mathematical ideas.

Depending on your school's homework policies and your own judgment, you may want to assign more homework than is suggested in the units. For this purpose you might use the practice pages, included as blackline masters at the end of this unit, to give students additional work with numbers.

For some homework assignments, you will want to adapt the activity to meet the needs of a variety of students in your class: those with special needs, those ready for more challenge, and second-language learners. You might change the numbers in a problem, make the activity more or less complex, or go through a sample activity with those who need extra help. You can modify any student sheet for either homework or class use. In particular, making numbers in a problem smaller or larger can make the same basic activity appropriate for a wider range of students.

Another issue to consider is how to handle the homework that students bring back to class—how to recognize the work they have done at home without spending too much time on it. Some teachers hold a short group discussion of different approaches to the assignment; others ask students to share and discuss their work with a neighbor, or post the homework around the room and give students time to tour it briefly. If you want to keep track of homework students bring in, be sure it ends up in a designated place.

Investigations at **Home** It is a good idea to make your policy on homework explicit to both students and their families when you begin teaching with *Investigations*. How frequently will you be assigning homework? When do you expect homework to be completed and brought back to school? What are your goals in assigning homework? How independent should families expect their children to be? What should the parent's or guardian's role be? The more explicit you can be about your expectations, the better the homework experience will be for everyone.

Investigations at Home (a booklet available separately for each unit, to send home with students) gives you a way to communicate with families about the work students are doing in class. This booklet includes a brief description of every session, a list of the mathematics content emphasized in each investigation, and a discussion of each homework assignment to help families more effectively support their children. Whether or not you are using the *Investigations* at Home booklets, we expect you to make your own choices about home-

work assignments. Feel free to omit any and to add extra ones you think are appropriate.

Family Letter A letter that you can send home to students' families is included with the blackline masters for each unit. Families need to be informed about the mathematics work in your classroom; they should be encouraged to participate in and support their children's work. A reminder to send home the letter for each unit appears in one of the early investigations. These letters are also available separately in Spanish, Vietnamese, Cantonese, Hmong, and Cambodian.

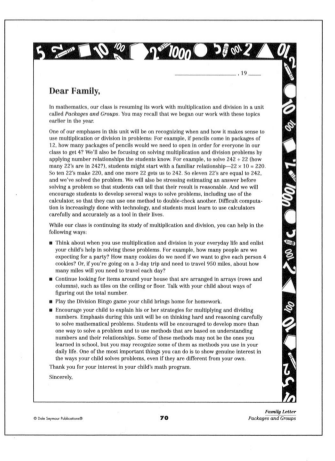

Help for You, the Teacher

Because we believe strongly that a new curriculum must help teachers think in new ways about mathematics and about their students' mathematical thinking processes, we have included a great deal of material to help you learn more about both.

About the Mathematics in This Unit This introductory section (p. I-17) summarizes the critical information about the mathematics you will be teaching. It describes the unit's central mathematical ideas and how students will encounter them through the unit's activities.

Teacher Notes These reference notes provide practical information about the mathematics you are teaching and about our experience with how students learn. Many of the notes were written in response to actual questions from teachers, or to discuss important things we saw happening in the field-test classrooms. Some teachers like to read them all before starting the unit, then review them as they come up in particular investigations.

Dialogue Boxes Sample dialogues demonstrate how students typically express their mathematical ideas, what issues and confusions arise in their thinking, and how some teachers have guided class discussions.

These dialogues are based on the extensive classroom testing of this curriculum; many are word-for-word transcriptions of recorded class discussions. They are not always easy reading; sometimes it may take some effort to unravel what the students are trying to say. But this is the value of these dialogues; they offer good clues to how your students may develop and express their approaches and strategies, helping you prepare for your own class discussions.

Where to Start You may not have time to read everything the first time you use this unit. As a first-time user, you will likely focus on understanding the activities and working them out with your students. Read completely through each investigation before starting to present it. Also read those sections listed in the Contents under the heading Where to Start (p. vi).

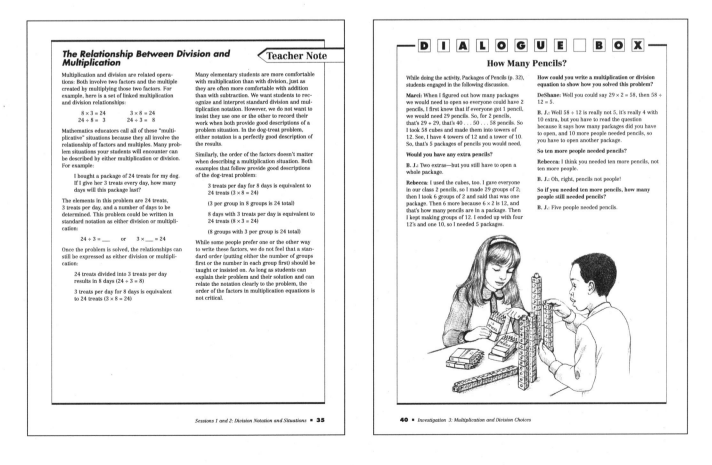

The Relationship Between Division and Multiplication
Teacher Note

Multiplication and division are related operations: Both involve two factors and the multiple created by multiplying those two factors. For example, here is a set of linked multiplication and division relationships:

$$8 \times 3 = 24 \qquad 3 \times 8 = 24$$
$$24 \div 8 = 3 \qquad 24 \div 3 = 8$$

Mathematics educators call all of these "multiplicative" situations because they all involve the relationship of factors and multiples. Many problem situations your students will encounter can be described by either multiplication or division. For example:

I bought a package of 24 treats for my dog. If I give her 3 treats every day, how many days will this package last?

The elements in this problem are 24 treats, 3 treats per day, and a number of days to be determined. This problem could be written in standard notation as either division or multiplication:

$$24 \div 3 = \_\_ \qquad \text{or} \qquad 3 \times \_\_ = 24$$

Once the problem is solved, the relationships can still be expressed as either division or multiplication:

24 treats divided into 3 treats per day results in 8 days ($24 \div 3 = 8$)

3 treats per day for 8 days is equivalent to 24 treats ($3 \times 8 = 24$)

Many elementary students are more comfortable with multiplication than with division, just as they are often more comfortable with addition than with subtraction. We want students to recognize and interpret standard division and multiplication notation. However, we do not want to insist they use one or the other to record their work when both provide good descriptions of a problem situation. In the dog-treat problem, either notation is a perfectly good description of the results.

Similarly, the order of the factors doesn't matter when describing a multiplication situation. Both examples that follow provide good descriptions of the dog-treat problem:

3 treats per day for 8 days is equivalent to 24 treats ($3 \times 8 = 24$)

(3 per group in 8 groups is 24 total)

8 days with 3 treats per day is equivalent to 24 treats ($8 \times 3 = 24$)

(8 groups with 3 per group is 24 total)

While some people prefer one or the other way to write these factors, we do not feel that a standard order (putting either the number of groups first or the number in each group first) should be taught or insisted on. As long as students can explain their problem and their solution and can relate the notation clearly to the problem, the order of the factors in multiplication equations is not critical.

D I A L O G U E   B O X

How Many Pencils?

While doing the activity, Packages of Pencils (p. 32), students engaged in the following discussion.

Marci: When I figured out how many packages we would need to open so everyone could have 2 pencils, I first knew that if everyone got 1 pencil, we would need 29 pencils. So, for 2 pencils, that's 29 + 29, that's 40 . . . 50 . . . 58 pencils. So I took 58 cubes and made them into towers of 12. See, I have 4 towers of 12 and a tower of 10. So, that's 5 packages of pencils you would need.

Would you have any extra pencils?

B. J.: Two extras—but you still have to open a whole package.

Rebecca: I used the cubes, too. I gave everyone in our class 2 pencils, so I made 29 groups of 2; then I took 6 groups of 2 and said that was one package. Then 6 more because 6 × 2 is 12, and that's how many pencils are in a package. Then I kept making groups of 12. I ended up with four 12's and one 10, so I needed 5 packages.

How could you write a multiplication or division equation to show how you solved this problem?

DeShane: Well you could say 29 × 2 = 58, then 58 ÷ 12 = 5.

B. J.: Well 58 ÷ 12 is really not 5, it's really 4 with 10 extra, but you have to read the question because it says how many packages did you have to open, and 10 more people needed pencils, so you have to open another package.

So ten more people needed pencils?

Rebecca: I think you needed ten more pencils, not ten more people.

B. J.: Oh, right, pencils not people!

So if you needed ten more pencils, how many people still needed pencils?

B. J.: Five people needed pencils.

The *Investigations* curriculum incorporates the use of two forms of technology in the classroom: calculators and computers. Calculators are assumed to be standard classroom materials, available for student use in any unit. Computers are explicitly linked to one or more units at each grade level; they are used with the unit on 2-D geometry at each grade, as well as with some of the units on measuring, data, and changes.

Using Calculators

In this curriculum, calculators are considered tools for doing mathematics, similar to pattern blocks or interlocking cubes. Just as with other tools, students must learn both *how* to use calculators correctly and *when* they are appropriate to use. This knowledge is crucial for daily life, as calculators are now a standard way of handling numerical operations, both at work and at home.

Using a calculator correctly is not a simple task; it depends on a good knowledge of the four operations and of the number system, so that students can select suitable calculations and also determine what a reasonable result would be. These skills are the basis of any work with numbers, whether or not a calculator is involved.

Unfortunately, calculators are often seen as tools to check computations with, as if other methods are somehow more fallible. Students need to understand that any computational method can be used to check any other; it's just as easy to make a mistake on the calculator as it is to make a mistake on paper or with mental arithmetic. Throughout this curriculum, we encourage students to solve computation problems in more than one way in order to double-check their accuracy. We present mental arithmetic, paper-and-pencil computation, and calculators as three possible approaches.

In this curriculum we also recognize that, despite their importance, calculators are not always appropriate in mathematics instruction. Like any tools, calculators are useful for some tasks, but not for others. You will need to make decisions about when to allow students access to calculators and when to ask that they solve problems without them, so that they can concentrate on other tools and skills. At times when calculators are or are not appropriate for a particular activity, we make specific recommendations. Help your students develop their own sense of which problems they can tackle with their own reasoning and which ones might be better solved with a combination of their own reasoning and the calculator.

Managing calculators in your classroom so that they are a tool, and not a distraction, requires some planning. When calculators are first introduced, students often want to use them for everything, even problems that can be solved quite simply by other methods. However, once the novelty wears off, students are just as interested in developing their own strategies, especially when these strategies are emphasized and valued in the classroom. Over time, students will come to recognize the ease and value of solving problems mentally, with paper and pencil, or with manipulatives, while also understanding the power of the calculator to facilitate work with larger numbers.

Experience shows that if calculators are available only occasionally, students become excited and distracted when they are permitted to use them. They focus on the tool rather than on the mathematics. In order to learn when calculators are appropriate and when they are not, students must have easy access to them and use them routinely in their work.

If you have a calculator for each student, and if you think your students can accept the responsibility, you might allow them to keep their calculators with the rest of their individual materials, at least for the first few weeks of school. Alternatively, you might store them in boxes on a shelf, number each calculator, and assign a corresponding number to each student. This system can give students a sense of ownership while also helping you keep track of the calculators.

Using Computers

Students can use computers to approach and visualize mathematical situations in new ways. The computer allows students to construct and manipulate geometric shapes, see objects move according to rules they specify, and turn, flip, and repeat a pattern.

This curriculum calls for computers in units where they are a particularly effective tool for learning mathematics content. One unit on 2-D geometry at each of the grades 3–5 includes a core of activities that rely on access to computers, either in the classroom or in a lab. Other units on geometry, measurement, data, and changes include computer activities, but can be taught without them. In these units, however, students' experience is greatly enhanced by computer use.

The following list outlines the recommended use of computers in this curriculum:

Grade 1
Unit: *Survey Questions and Secret Rules*
   (Collecting and Sorting Data)
Software: Tabletop, Jr.
Source: Broderbund

Unit: *Quilt Squares and Block Towns*
   (2-D and 3-D Geometry)
Software: *Shapes*
Source: provided with the unit

Grade 2
Unit: *Mathematical Thinking at Grade 2*
   (Introduction)
Software: *Shapes*
Source: provided with the unit

Unit: *Shapes, Halves, and Symmetry*
   (Geometry and Fractions)
Software: *Shapes*
Source: provided with the unit

Unit: *How Long? How Far?* (Measuring)
Software: *Geo-Logo*
Source: provided with the unit

Grade 3
Unit: *Flips, Turns, and Area* (2-D Geometry)
Software: *Tumbling Tetrominoes*
Source: provided with the unit

Unit: *Turtle Paths* (2-D Geometry)
Software: *Geo-Logo*
Source: provided with the unit

Grade 4
Unit: *Sunken Ships and Grid Patterns*
   (2-D Geometry)
Software: *Geo-Logo*
Source: provided with the unit

Grade 5
Unit: *Picturing Polygons* (2-D Geometry)
Software: *Geo-Logo*
Source: provided with the unit

Unit: *Patterns of Change* (Tables and Graphs)
Software: *Trips*
Source: provided with the unit

Unit: *Data: Kids, Cats, and Ads* (Statistics)
Software: Tabletop, Sr.
Source: Broderbund

The software provided with the *Investigations* units uses the power of the computer to help students explore mathematical ideas and relationships that cannot be explored in the same way with physical materials. With the *Shapes* (grades 1–2) and *Tumbling Tetrominoes* (grade 3) software, students explore symmetry, pattern, rotation and reflection, area, and characteristics of 2-D shapes. With the *Geo-Logo* software (grades 3–5), students investigate rotations and reflections, coordinate geometry, the properties of 2-D shapes, and angles. The *Trips* software (grade 5) is a mathematical exploration of motion in which students run experiments and interpret data presented in graphs and tables.

We suggest that students work in pairs on the computer; this not only maximizes computer resources but also encourages students to consult, monitor, and teach one another. Generally, more than two students at one computer find it difficult to share. Managing access to computers is an issue for every classroom. The curriculum gives you explicit support for setting up a system. The units are structured on the assumption that you have enough computers for half your students to work on the machines in pairs at one time. If you do not have access to that many computers, suggestions are made for structuring class time to use the unit with five to eight computers, or even with fewer than five.

Assessment plays a critical role in teaching and learning, and it is an integral part of the *Investigations* curriculum. For a teacher using these units, assessment is an ongoing process. You observe students' discussions and explanations of their strategies on a daily basis and examine their work as it evolves. While students are busy recording and representing their work, working on projects, sharing with partners, and playing mathematical games, you have many opportunities to observe their mathematical thinking. What you learn through observation guides your decisions about how to proceed. In any of the units, you will repeatedly consider questions like these:

■ Do students come up with their own strategies for solving problems, or do they expect others to tell them what to do? What do their strategies reveal about their mathematical understanding?

■ Do students understand that there are different strategies for solving problems? Do they articulate their strategies and try to understand other students' strategies?

■ How effectively do students use materials as tools to help with their mathematical work?

■ Do students have effective ideas for keeping track of and recording their work? Does keeping track of and recording their work seem difficult for them?

You will need to develop a comfortable and efficient system for recording and keeping track of your observations. Some teachers keep a clipboard handy and jot notes on a class list or on adhesive labels that are later transferred to student files. Others keep loose-leaf notebooks with a page for each student and make weekly notes about what they have observed in class.

Assessment Tools in the Unit

With the activities in each unit, you will find questions to guide your thinking while observing the students at work. You will also find two built-in assessment tools: Teacher Checkpoints and embedded Assessment activities.

Teacher Checkpoints The designated Teacher Checkpoints in each unit offer a time to "check in" with individual students, watch them at work, and ask questions that illuminate how they are thinking.

At first it may be hard to know what to look for, hard to know what kinds of questions to ask. Students may be reluctant to talk; they may not be accustomed to having the teacher ask them about their work, or they may not know how to explain their thinking. Two important ingredients of this process are asking students open-ended questions about their work and showing genuine interest in how they are approaching the task. When students see that you are interested in their thinking and are counting on them to come up with their own ways of solving problems, they may surprise you with the depth of their understanding.

Teacher Checkpoints also give you the chance to pause in the teaching sequence and reflect on how your class is doing overall. Think about whether you need to adjust your pacing: Are most students fluent with strategies for solving a particular kind of problem? Are they just starting to formulate good strategies? Or are they still struggling with how to start? Depending on what you see as the students work, you may want to spend more time on similar problems, change some of the problems to use smaller numbers, move quickly to more challenging material, modify subsequent activities for some students, work on particular ideas with a small group, or pair students who have good strategies with those who are having more difficulty.

Embedded Assessment Activities Assessment activities embedded in each unit will help you examine specific pieces of student work, figure out what it means, and provide feedback. From the students' point of view, these assessment activities are no different from any others. Each is a learning experience in and of itself, as well as an opportunity for you to gather evidence about students' mathematical understanding.

The embedded assessment activities sometimes involve writing and reflecting; at other times, a discussion or brief interaction between student and teacher; and in still other instances, the creation and explanation of a product. In most cases, the assessments require that students *show* what they did, *write* or *talk* about it, or do both. Having to explain how they worked through a problem helps students be more focused and clear in their mathematical thinking. It also helps them realize that doing mathematics is a process that may involve tentative starts, revising one's approach, taking different paths, and working through ideas.

Teachers often find the hardest part of assessment to be interpreting their students' work. We provide guidelines to help with that interpretation. If you have used a process approach to teaching writing, the assessment in *Investigations* will seem familiar. For many of the assessment activities, a Teacher Note provides examples of student work and a commentary on what it indicates about student thinking.

Documentation of Student Growth

To form an overall picture of mathematical progress, it is important to document each student's work in journals, notebooks, or portfolios. The choice is largely a matter of personal preference; some teachers have students keep a notebook or folder for each unit, while others prefer one mathematics notebook, or a portfolio of selected work for the entire year. The final activity in each *Investigations* unit, called Choosing Student Work to Save, helps you and the students select representative samples for a record of their work.

This kind of regular documentation helps you synthesize information about each student as a mathematical learner. From different pieces of evidence, you can put together the big picture. This synthesis will be invaluable in thinking about where to go next with a particular child, deciding where more work is needed, or explaining to parents (or other teachers) how a child is doing.

If you use portfolios, you need to collect a good balance of work, yet avoid being swamped with an overwhelming amount of paper. Following are some tips for effective portfolios:

- Collect a representative sample of work, including some pieces that students themselves select for inclusion in the portfolio. There should be just a few pieces for each unit, showing different kinds of work—some assignments that involve writing, as well as some that do not.

- If students do not date their work, do so yourself so that you can reconstruct the order in which pieces were done.

- Include your reflections on the work. When you are looking back over the whole year, such comments are reminders of what seemed especially interesting about a particular piece; they can also be helpful to other teachers and to parents. Older students should be encouraged to write their own reflections about their work.

Assessment Overview

There are two places to turn for a preview of the assessment opportunities in each *Investigations* unit. The Assessment Resources column in the unit Overview Chart (pp. I-13–I-15) identifies the Teacher Checkpoints and Assessment activities embedded in each investigation, guidelines for observing the students that appear within classroom activities, and any Teacher Notes and Dialogue Boxes that explain what to look for and what types of student responses you might expect to see in your classroom. Additionally, the section About the Assessment in This Unit (p. I-18) gives you a detailed list of questions for each investigation, keyed to the mathematical emphases, to help you observe student growth.

Depending on your situation, you may want to provide additional assessment opportunities. Most of the investigations lend themselves to more frequent assessment, simply by having students do more writing and recording while they are working.

Packages and Groups

Content of This Unit   Students continue to build on their understanding of multiplication and division, extending concepts and skills studied earlier in the year in *Arrays and Shares*. They use 300 charts, rectangular arrays, games, and calculators and begin to develop theories about finding factors of large numbers. Students work on learning single-digit multiplication pairs. They continue to develop and refine their strategies, based on what they know about numbers, to solve multi-digit multiplication and division problems.

Connections with Other Units If you are doing the full-year *Investigations* curriculum in the suggested sequence for Grade 4, this is the ninth of eleven units. Your class will already have had experience with skip counting, multiplication and division, and the composition of large numbers through their work in the units *Arrays and Shares* and *Landmarks in the Thousands*.

Note: The unit *Arrays and Shares* is a prerequisite for the work students will be doing in *Packages and Groups*. Some of the materials used in *Arrays and Shares*—namely, the Array Cards, sets A and B, and the array transparencies—are needed also for *Packages and Groups*.

If your school is not using the full-year curriculum, this unit can also be used successfully at grade 5.

Investigations Curriculum ■ Suggested Grade 4 Sequence

Mathematical Thinking at Grade 4 (Introduction)

Arrays and Shares (Multiplication and Division)

Seeing Solids and Silhouettes (3-D Geometry)

Landmarks in the Thousands (The Number System)

Different Shapes, Equal Pieces (Fractions and Area)

The Shape of the Data (Statistics)

Money, Miles, and Large Numbers (Addition and Subtraction)

Changes Over Time (Graphs)

▶ *Packages and Groups* (Multiplication and Division)

Sunken Ships and Grid Patterns (2-D Geometry)

Three out of Four Like Spaghetti (Data and Fractions)

Investigation 1 ▪ Multiplication Tables

Class Sessions	Activities	Pacing
Sessions 1 and 2 (p. 4) MAKING A MULTIPLICATION TABLE	Making a Multiplication Table Using Arrays Discussing the Multiplication Tables Discussing Difficult Multiplication Pairs Homework: Making a Multiplication Table Extension: Another Pattern	minimum 2 hr
Session 3 (Excursion)* (p. 9) MULTIPLE PLAIDS	Finding Multiples on the Multiplication Table Extension: Multiple Patterns	minimum 1 hr
Sessions 4 and 5 (p. 11) MULTIPLES OF LARGER NUMBERS	Skip Counting by Two-Digit Numbers Making a Multiple Tower Teacher Checkpoint: Multiple Towers and Working on Difficult Pairs Homework: Making Multiple Towers Extension: Comparing Numbers in Multiple Towers	minimum 2 hr

◗ **Ten-Minute Math** ▪ **Exploring Data**

*Excursions can be omitted without harming the integrity or continuity of the unit, but offer good mathematical work if you have time to include them.

Mathematical Emphasis

- Looking for and using the multiplication patterns of numbers (for example, students identify multiples of 5 by checking that the units digit is either a 5 or a 0)

- Becoming familiar with the multiples of larger numbers (for example, skip counting by double-digit numbers, such as 25)

- Identifying factors of larger numbers

Assessment Resources

Using Patterns to Make the Multiplication Table (Dialogue Box, p. 8)

Teacher Checkpoint: Multiple Towers and Working on Difficult Pairs (p. 13)

Building a Multiple Tower (Dialogue Box, p. 15)

Materials

Array Cards

Scissors

Crayons or markers

Calculators

Interlocking cubes

Stick-on notes or index cards

Tape or glue sticks

Adding machine tape

Overhead projector

Student Sheets 1–2

Teaching resource sheets

Family letter

Investigation 2 ▪ Double-Digit Multiplication

Class Sessions	Activities	Pacing
Session 1 (p. 18) MULTIPLYING TWO-DIGIT NUMBERS	Returning to Multiplication Clusters Making a Cluster of Problems Homework: A Cluster of Problems	minimum 1 hr
Sessions 2 and 3 (p. 24) SOLVING AND CREATING CLUSTER PROBLEMS	Making Close Estimates Teacher Checkpoint: Solving a Problem in Two Ways Making a Cluster of Problems Homework: More Cluster Problems Homework: Other People's Strategies	minimum 2 hr

◔ **Ten-Minute Math** ▪ **Exploring Data**

Mathematical Emphasis

- Using familiar landmark numbers to solve problems (for example, determining whether the solution is greater than 100, 200, 300, and so on)

- Partitioning large numbers to multiply them more easily (for example, 24×8 is thought of as $[20 \times 8] + [4 \times 8]$)

- Solving double-digit multiplication problems (for example, 32×21)

Assessment Resources

About Cluster Problems (Teacher Note, p. 21)

Solving 42×8 (Dialogue Box, p. 22)

Writing About Cluster Problems (Teacher Note, p. 23)

Teacher Checkpoint: Solving a Problem in Two Ways (p. 25)

Materials

Calculators

Interlocking cubes

Overhead projector

Blank transparencies

Stick-on notes

Student Sheets 3–8

Investigation 3 ▪ Multiplication and Division Choices

Class Sessions	Activities	Pacing
Sessions 1 and 2 (p. 30) DIVISION NOTATION AND SITUATIONS	How Many 4's in 48? Teacher Checkpoint: Connecting Division Equations to a Context Packages of Pencils Homework: More Pencil Problems	minimum 2 hr
Session 3 (p. 41) LOOKING MORE CLOSELY AT DIVISION PROBLEMS	Dividing by Grouping Another Problem with Cubes Homework: Guess My Number Problems	minimum 1 hr
Sessions 4, 5, and 6 (p. 46) CHOICE TIME	Assessment: 34×12 Choice Time Class Discussion: Marvin's Mystery Multiple Tower Class Discussion: Strategies for Solving Difficult Two-Digit Division Problems Homework: Marvin's Mystery Multiple Tower	minimum 3 hr
Sessions 7 and 8 (p. 51) WHAT ARE NUMBERS DIVISIBLE BY?	Marbles in a Bag Looking for Relationships Finding Factors of Large Numbers Class Discussion: Making Conjectures About Finding Factors Homework: Finding Factors Extension: Which Numbers Have Many Factors?	minimum 2 hr
Session 9 (p. 56) DIVISION BINGO	Testing Out Conjectures Introducing Division Bingo on the Multiplication Table Playing Division Bingo Homework: Division Bingo	minimum 1 hr
Session 10 (p. 60) ASSESSING STUDENTS' UNDERSTANDING OF DIVISION	Assessment: $287 \div 14$ Division Bingo Choosing Student Work to Save	minimum 1 hr

◖ **Ten-Minute Math** ▪ **Guess My Number**

Mathematical Emphasis

- Understanding how division notation can represent a variety of division situations (including sharing and grouping situations)

- Creating a context that is representative of a division equation

- Using familiar landmark numbers to solve problems

- Using multiplication and division relationships to solve problems

- Exploring factors of large numbers (including triple-digit numbers) and developing conjectures about divisibility

- Finding multiples

Assessment Resources

Teacher Checkpoint: Connecting Division Equations to a Context (p. 31)

Observing the Students (pp. 33, 44, 58)

The Relationship Between Division and Multiplication (Teacher Note, p. 35)

What About Notation? (Teacher Note, p. 36)

Two Kinds of Division: Sharing and Partitioning (Teacher Note, p. 37)

What Do You Do with the Remainders? (Teacher Note, p. 39)

How Many Pencils? (Dialogue Box, p. 40)

Different Ways to Do Division (Teacher Note, p. 45)

Assessment: 34×12 (p. 46); $287 \div 14$ (p. 60)

Choosing Student Work to Save (p. 62)

Materials

Calculators

Interlocking cubes

Box or container

Paper cups or plates

Tape or glue stick

Graph paper

Stick-on notes or index cards

Adding machine tape

Chart paper

Scissors

Crayons or markers

Overhead projector

Blank transparencies

Student Sheets 9–20

Teaching resource sheets

Following are the basic materials needed for the activities in this unit. Many of the items can be purchased from the publisher, either individually or in the Teacher Resource Package and the Student Materials Kit for grade 4. Detailed information is available on the *Investigations* order form. To obtain this form, call toll-free 1-800-872-1100 and ask for a Dale Seymour customer service representative.

Snap™ Cubes (interlocking cubes): at least 128 per pair

Calculators: 1 per student, if possible

Adding machine tape

Graph paper

Large poster or chart paper: 1 sheet per pair of students, plus extras

Crayons or markers

Box or container filled with 128 cubes

Paper cups or plates: at least 20

Array Cards, Sets A and B (manufactured), or use the Array Cards students made in the unit *Arrays and Shares*: 1 set per student

Stick-on notes or index cards: about 90 per student

Chart paper: 1–2 sheets per pair

Tape or glue sticks

Scissors

Overhead projector

Blank transparencies

The following materials are provided at the end of this unit as blackline masters. A Student Activity Booklet containing all student sheets and teaching resources needed for individual work is available.

Family Letter (p. 70)

Student Sheets 1–20 (p. 71)

Teaching Resources:

   Number Cards (p. 97)

   Completed Multiplication Table (p. 98)

   300 Chart (p. 99)

Practice Pages (p. 101)

Related Children's Literature

Birch, David. *The King's Chessboard.* New York: Dial Books for Young Readers, 1988.

Dahl, Roald. *Esio Trot.* New York: Puffin Books, 1990.

This unit continues to build on the concepts introduced earlier in the year in the unit *Arrays and Shares*. Central to students' understanding the processes and applications of multiplication and division is the ability to create a mental image of the operation. This becomes especially important as students begin to work with larger numbers. Where skip counting by a number may be a perfectly appropriate strategy for calculating 8×6, it is a cumbersome strategy for solving 34×21. It is important that students have an image of "21 groups of 34" and that they use their knowledge of numbers to find ways of calculating and combining familiar groups, such as: 10 groups of 34 is equal to 340, 20 groups is double that (680), then add one more group of 34 to get 714.

Similarly, when students encounter a division problem such as $242 \div 22$, they need first to be able to interpret the problem as "How many groups of 22 are in 242?" or "If 242 things were shared by 22 people, how many would each person get?" When students begin to deal with larger numbers, it is important they have a grouping (measuring) model of division as well as a sharing model to work with. In this situation it would be quite difficult actually to deal out items into 22 groups. Students need to be able to think about the problem in terms of "taking out groups of 22."

The focus of this unit is on supporting students to make sense out of multiplication and division and to develop strong images of what happens when numbers are multiplied or divided. Reinforcing their knowledge of multiplication pairs (also known as multiplication facts), strengthening their ability to break apart problems into more familiar parts ($23 \times 7 = 20 \times 7 + 3 \times 7$), and deepening their understanding of the composition of numbers are important parts of their foundation of understanding. Each of these plays a critical part in students being able to keep track of all the important components of a multiplication or division problem involving multi-digit numbers.

One of the reasons students have traditionally been taught complicated algorithms early is because they are a way of keeping track of all the components of a problem. However, if students merely memorize these procedures without any understanding or visual image of what they represent or why they make sense, they are limited in their ability to interpret problems and judge the reasonableness of their answers.

Students do need to develop efficient computational strategies, many of which will be mental strategies, but these must be based on their understanding of quantities and their relationships. We would like to see students solving problems using number sense, estimation, and strategies built on an understanding of the number relationships involved in the problem.

Mathematical Emphasis At the beginning of each investigation, the Mathematical Emphasis section tells you what is most important for students to learn during that investigation. Many of these mathematical understandings and processes are difficult and complex. Students gradually learn more and more about each idea over many years of schooling. Individual students will begin and end the unit with different levels of knowledge and skill, but all will gain greater knowledge about the processes and applications of multiplication and division.

Throughout the *Investigations* curriculum, there are many opportunities for ongoing daily assessment as you observe, listen to, and interact with students at work. In this unit, you will find three Teacher Checkpoints:

Investigation 1, Sessions 4–5:
Multiple Towers and Working on Difficult Pairs (p. 13)

Investigation 2, Sessions 2–3:
Solving a Problem in Two Ways (p. 25)

Investigation 3, Sessions 1–2:
Connecting Division Equations to a Context (p. 31)

This unit also has two embedded assessment activities:

Investigation 3, Sessions 4–6:
34×12 (p. 46)

Investigation 3, Session 10:
$287 \div 14$ (p. 60)

In addition, you can use almost any activity in this unit to assess your students' needs and strengths. Listed below are questions to help you focus your observation in each investigation. You may want to keep track of your observations for each student to help you plan your curriculum and monitor students' growth. Suggestions for documenting student growth can be found in the section About Assessment (p. I-10).

Investigation 1: Multiplication Tables

- What patterns do students notice in the multiplication tables? Do they use them? How?

- Can students skip count by larger numbers, such as 25 or 36? How comfortable are they with multiples of such numbers?

- How do students identify factors of larger numbers? Do they use their experience with skip counting? Do they understand the relationship between factors and multiples?

Investigation 2: Double-Digit Multiplication

- What strategies do students use to estimate and solve multiplication problems? Do they use landmark numbers? repeated addition? Do they partition larger problems into smaller, more manageable parts (such as breaking 24×8 into $[20 \times 8] + [4 \times 8]$)? Do they use familiar multiplication combinations to solve unfamiliar problems?

Investigation 3: Multiplication and Division Choices

- How do students interpret problems presented with division notation? Do they understand that division notation can represent a variety of division situations (including sharing and grouping situations)?

- How do students invent contexts for a given division equation? Do they create only sharing situations? (For example, how much would each person get if I share $152 fairly among 4 people?) only grouping situations? (For example, I have 152 apples, and packages hold 4 apples. How many packages do I need?) Do they use a particular context to make sense of any remainders? How?

- How do students use familiar landmark numbers (for example, by estimating 32×9 as 30×10, or about 300, or solving 32×9 by multiplying 32×10 and then subtracting 32)?

- What strategies are students using to solve multiplication and division problems? Do they use relationships between multiplication and division? How?

- How do students determine the factors of larger numbers? How do they develop and test conjectures about divisibility?

- How do students find multiples of larger numbers? What patterns do students notice? Do they use them? How?

In the *Investigations* curriculum, mathematical vocabulary is introduced naturally during the activities. We don't ask students to learn definitions of new terms; rather, they come to understand such words as *factor*, *area*, and *symmetry* by hearing them used frequently in discussion as they investigate new concepts. This approach is compatible with current theories of second-language acquisition, which emphasize the use of new vocabulary in meaningful contexts while students are actively involved with objects, pictures, and physical movement.

Listed below are some key words used in this unit that will not be new to most English speakers at this age level, but may be unfamiliar to students with limited English proficiency. You will want to spend additional time working on these words with your students who are learning English. If your students are working with a second-language teacher, you might enlist your colleague's aid in familiarizing students with these words before and during this unit. In the classroom, look for opportunities for students to hear and use these words. Activities you can use to present the words are given in the appendix, Vocabulary Support for Second-Language Learners (p. 67).

tower Students generate lists of multiples for a given number. They record these multiples on cards or stick-on notes and build a Multiple Tower as tall as they are. Students are encouraged to look for patterns in their lists of multiples as a way of predicting what number will come next.

extra Students deal with division problems that do not always divide evenly. In these situations, students must make a decision about what to do with the remainders or extras. Students are encouraged to describe the remainder in the context of the problem.

Multicultural Extensions for All Students

Whenever possible, encourage students to share words, objects, customs, or any aspects of daily life from their own cultures and backgrounds that are relevant to the activities in this unit. For example:

- When students are making up problem situations that represent division situations, encourage them to write problems that are based on aspects of their cultures—foods, games, objects, sports that involve teams, and so forth.

Investigations

Multiplication Tables

What Happens

Sessions 1 and 2: Making a Multiplication Table Using Array Cards, students make multiplication tables. As they fill in their tables, they look for patterns that they then discuss. In pairs or small groups, students discuss and list difficult multiplication pairs. They share strategies for learning these "difficult pairs."

Session 3 (Excursion): Multiple Plaids Students look for patterns on the multiplication tables by highlighting multiples of different numbers. They work in groups to create a set of tables for multiples 2 through 12 and then write statements about the patterns they observe for each multiple.

Sessions 4 and 5: Multiples of Larger Numbers Students use cubes, 300 charts, and calculators as tools to skip count by larger numbers. They make lists of the multiples of these numbers and look for patterns in these multiples. They make Multiple Towers and work on learning some of the multiplication pairs that are difficult for them.

Mathematical Emphasis

- Looking for and using the multiplication patterns of numbers (for example, students identify multiples of 5 by checking that the units digit is either a 5 or a 0)

- Becoming familiar with the multiples of larger numbers (for example, skip counting by double-digit numbers, such as 25)

- Identifying factors of larger numbers

What to Plan Ahead of Time

Materials

- Array Cards, Sets A and B (If you haven't purchased the manufactured cards, students can use the Array Cards they made in the unit *Arrays and Shares* or they can make new sets from the blackline masters in that unit.) (Sessions 1–2)

- Overhead transparencies of the Array Cards (made for the unit *Arrays and Shares*) (Sessions 1–2)

- Scissors (Sessions 1–2)

- Crayons or markers (Excursion, Sessions 4–5)

- Calculators: at least 1 per pair of students (Sessions 4–5)

- Interlocking cubes: at least 50–60 per student (Sessions 4–5)

- Stick-on notes or index cards: 50–60 per student (Sessions 4–5)

- Tape or glue sticks (Sessions 4–5)

- Adding machine tape: 1 roll; or strips of oak tag (Sessions 4–5)

- Overhead projector (Sessions 1–5)

Other Preparation

- Duplicate student sheets and teaching resources, located at the end of this unit, in the following quantities. If you have Student Activity Booklets, copy only the items marked with an asterisk, including any extra materials and transparencies needed.

For Sessions 1–2

Student Sheet 1, Making a Multiplication Table (p. 71): 1 per student (class), 1 per student (homework), some extras* in case of mistakes, and 1 overhead transparency*

Family letter* (p. 70): 1 per student. Remember to sign and date it before copying.

For Session 3

Completed Multiplication Table (p. 98): 4 per student, and 1 overhead transparency*

Student Sheet 1, Making a Multiplication Table (p. 71): 1 per student, optional

For Sessions 4–5

Student Sheet 2, Making Multiple Towers (p. 72): 1 per student (homework)

300 chart (p. 99): 3 per student

- Begin to make a multiplication table for yourself using the arrays and a blank multiplication table (Student Sheet 1) as described in Session 1.

- Assemble (or have the students assemble) your interlocking cubes in columns of ten. Insist that the students return cubes in columns of ten when they are finished using them.

- If you plan to provide folders in which students will save their work for the entire unit, prepare these for distribution during Session 1.

Making a Multiplication Table

Materials

- Array Cards, Sets A and B
- Transparencies of arrays
- Student Sheet 1 (at least 2 per student)
- Transparency of Student Sheet 1
- Overhead projector
- Scissors (optional)
- Family Letter

What Happens

Using Array Cards, students make multiplication tables. As they fill in their tables, they look for patterns that they then discuss. In pairs or small groups, students discuss and list difficult multiplication pairs. They share strategies for learning these "difficult pairs." Their work focuses on:

- constructing multiplication tables from arrays
- looking for patterns in the multiplication tables

Activity

Making a Multiplication Table Using Arrays

Students will need their Array Cards and blank multiplication tables (Student Sheet 1). On the overhead projector, model the procedure for making a multiplication table. Use the overhead arrays from the unit *Arrays and Shares* and the overhead transparency of Student Sheet 1, Making a Multiplication Table.

Choose one array. Fit the array, total side up, in the upper-left corner of the grid. Notice that the corner square is marked with a dot. This will help the children orient their arrays on the paper. Find the lower-right corner square of the array and lift it up; and in the corresponding square of the paper, write the total of that array.

Next, rotate the array so length becomes width and width becomes length; lift up the lower-right corner square and write the total of that array in the corresponding square of the paper.

Repeat this using another array. When the totals of the arrays are recorded on the grid, a multiplication table is created. Have the whole class do two or three of the same arrays together. Remind students to align their arrays correctly on the tables.

Using Patterns to Fill in the Tables Students work in pairs or small groups to complete the multiplication tables. They need not use their arrays to fill in the entire table. Encourage them to look for patterns in entries already made and to use these patterns to complete rows and columns of their tables.

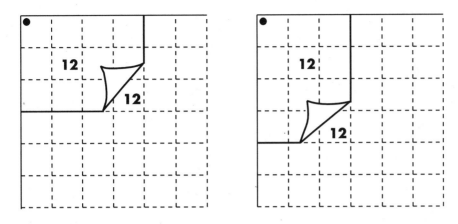

When students have completed most of their tables, have them compare tables with their partners or group members and discuss any numbers that are not the same. The following discussion on patterns will be more meaningful to students if their tables are correct.

As you walk around, notice how students are filling in their tables. As you interact with individuals or small groups, the following questions can help to focus their attention on the overall formation of the multiplication tables:

Do you see any patterns?

What symmetry do you see in this multiplication table?

Pick an empty square. Can you predict which number will go in it?

If you notice a pattern, follow it through by writing lightly the numbers you think go in some of the empty boxes. Test your conjectures with other arrays.

Do some numbers appear more often than others? Which ones?

Questions students explore will depend on what their tables look like and on what arrays they have chosen to record first. See the **Dialogue Box**, Using Patterns to Make the Multiplication Table (p. 8).

Note: At the end of Session 1, assign the homework explained on p. 7.

Activity

Using the overhead transparency of Student Sheet 1, show students how this is a multiplication table. By choosing a number from the left side and a number from the top and following them across and down with their fingers until their fingers intersect, they can find the product of those numbers.

Discussing the Multiplication Tables

As a class, students discuss how they filled in their multiplication tables. Some students may have used patterns to fill in the tables, others may have computed each multiplication problem. Encourage those students who used patterns to share how they filled in the table. (If students also have completed their second multiplication table for homework, they can consider that one as well.)

Look at the multiplication table you made yesterday or last night for homework. How did you fill in your table?

What did you notice about your table?

Make a list of student observations.

Where are the smaller numbers? The larger numbers? Why do you suppose that is?

If students don't mention the line of symmetry, point it out.

Do you see a line of symmetry on your table? What's special about the numbers on it?

The line of symmetry is where the same patterns of numbers fall on either side of the line. On the multiplication table, the line of symmetry is the left-to-right diagonal (beginning at 1 and going to 144). It runs through the square numbers (1, 4, 9, 16, 25, etc.). If students have cut out their tables into a 12 × 12 square, they can fold the table along the diagonal to see the line of symmetry.

Pose the following question for students to explore.

Some numbers occur more often than others on the table. Which ones?

Why do you think that is? Are they related in any way?

Start a list on the board of some numbers and the number of occurrences.

Discussing Difficult Multiplication Pairs

Using both their multiplication tables and their Array Cards, students work with partners to compile a list of the multiplication pairs they feel are the most difficult. You might suggest students sort their arrays into two piles, one pile of "pairs I know" and the other pile of "pairs I am still working on." As they discuss these lists with their partners, encourage students to share strategies with each other for learning difficult pairs.

At the end of this session and periodically throughout the unit, give students five minutes to practice difficult pairs with partners. This can be done at any time during the day or could be integrated into a homework assignment.

Students should tape their multiplication tables on the outside of their math folders so they can be used as references at any time.

Sessions 1 and 2 Follow-Up

Making a Multiplication Table   After Session 1, students make a second multiplication table (without looking at the multiplication table made in class) for homework. Students can fill in rows and columns in order using the patterns they noticed when making the first table. They can use arrays as a back-up to fill in cells they find difficult. Each student will need another blank multiplication table (Student Sheet 1). Since the unit *Arrays and Shares* is a prerequisite to this unit, students should already have a set of Array Cards at home from their work in that unit.

Send home the family letter or the *Investigations* at Home booklet with this homework assignment. Remember to sign and date the letter before copying it.

Another Pattern   Students investigate which numbers on the multiplication table occur an odd number of times and which numbers occur an even number of times. Students are likely to notice that on the multiplication table square numbers (1, 4, 9, 16) occur an odd number of times. Encourage them to explain why this happens.

 **Homework**

Extension

DIALOGUE BOX

Using Patterns to Make the Multiplication Table

As students were completing the activity Making a Multiplication Table Using Arrays (p. 4), they made these observations:

Nadim: Hey, the pattern of numbers is the same even if you turn it like this. The numbers happen on both sides of the diagonal. Look, the numbers on the diagonal are 49, 64, 81 . . . that's 7 × 7, and 8 × 8, and 9 × 9. I can just fill in the rest.

[*Nadim fills in all the square numbers under 81.*]

Nadim: I wonder what the largest square number is on this sheet? Let's see, it's 12 squares wide, so it's 12 × 12.

[*Nadim uses the calculator to compute the total and fills in 144 in the square at the bottom right end of the diagonal.*]

Tuong: I counted by 5's to fill in the 5's row: 5, 10, 15, 20, 25, 30. It works going across and going down. The 2's row and column works the same way. See?

Nick: I noticed that the biggest numbers are farthest away from the dot. I can also tell where the total would go without using the array. I just think about the sides of the rectangle and go across and then down, and that square is where the total goes.

Teresa: I noticed what Tuong noticed. Each row going down has one like it going across. If I have two numbers in a row, I can figure out what the next one will be by counting how much is between each number. Twenty-four to 30 is [*counting on her fingers*] 25, 26, 27, 28, 29 . . . 6. There's 6 from 24 to 30, so the next one is 36, and the next one is [*counts on her fingers*] 42.

Multiple Plaids

What Happens

Students look for patterns on multiplication tables by highlighting multiples of different numbers. They work in groups to create a set of tables for multiples 2 through 12 and then write statements about the patterns they observe for each multiple. Their work focuses on:

- finding sets of multiples in different tables
- finding more patterns in the multiplication table

Materials

- Completed Multiplication Table (4 per student)
- Markers or crayons
- Transparency of Completed Multiplication Table
- Student Sheet 1 (1 per student, optional)
- Overhead projector

Activity

Finding Multiples on the Multiplication Table

Pass out four copies of the Completed Multiplication Table to each student to color in patterns. You will need an overhead transparency of this sheet.

I'm going to color in all the multiples of 6. Multiples of 6 are the numbers we say when we skip count by 6. Let's count around the class by 6's.

As the students count by 6's, record the multiples on the board as they say them. If your students have done the Ten-Minute Math, Counting Around the Class, they will be familiar with this process.

Where on the multiplication table do you see multiples of 6?

Take a few suggestions and color them on the overhead. Students color in the multiples of 6 on their tables at the same time.

Multiples of 6

1	2	3	4	5	6	7	8	9	10	11	12
2	4	6	8	10	12	14	16	18	20	22	24
3	6	9	12	15	18	21	24	27	30	33	36
4	8	12	16	20	24	28	32	36	40	44	48
5	10	15	20	25	30	35	40	45	50	55	60
6	12	18	24	30	36	42	48	54	60	66	72
7	14	21	28	35	42	49	56	63	70	77	84
8	16	24	32	40	48	56	64	72	80	88	96
9	18	27	36	45	54	63	72	81	90	99	108
10	20	30	40	50	60	70	80	90	100	110	120
11	22	33	44	55	66	77	88	99	110	121	132
12	24	36	48	60	72	84	96	108	120	132	144

Multiples of 5

1	2	3	4	5	6	7	8	9	10	11	12
2	4	6	8	10	12	14	16	18	20	22	24
3	6	9	12	15	18	21	24	27	30	33	36
4	8	12	16	20	24	28	32	36	40	44	48
5	10	15	20	25	30	35	40	45	50	55	60
6	12	18	24	30	36	42	48	54	60	66	72
7	14	21	28	35	42	49	56	63	70	77	84
8	16	24	32	40	48	56	64	72	80	88	96
9	18	27	36	45	54	63	72	81	90	99	108
10	20	30	40	50	60	70	80	90	100	110	120
11	22	33	44	55	66	77	88	99	110	121	132
12	24	36	48	60	72	84	96	108	120	132	144

Working in groups of four, have students color in the multiples of 2, 3, 4, and 5, each on a different multiplication table. Each group member should choose a different set of multiples to color so the group has a set of tables to compare. As each group finishes, the members discuss the patterns they see on their tables. Each group decides on one or two statements to write below each table about the patterns they notice.

Groups continue coloring patterns and writing statements for the multiples of 8, 9, 10, and 12. Groups that finish early can color tables for the multiples of 7 and 11.

Discussing Multiple Patterns   In a whole-class discussion, ask students:

What patterns did you notice? What other tables did the multiples of 3 show up in?

Session 3 Follow-Up

Extension

Multiple Patterns   Each student chooses a number and colors in the multiples of that number on a blank multiplication table (Student Sheet 1), *without* filling in the numbers. Students exchange colored tables and try to guess which set of multiples the pattern represents.

Multiples of Larger Numbers

What Happens

Students use cubes, 300 charts, and calculators as tools to skip count by larger numbers. They make lists of the multiples of these numbers and look for patterns in these multiples. They make Multiple Towers and work on learning some of the multiplication pairs that are difficult for them. Their work focuses on:

- skip counting by two-digit numbers
- finding multiples of larger numbers

 Ten-Minute Math: Exploring Data Once or twice in the next few days, do Exploring Data. This activity can be done during any free ten minutes during the day.

You or the students decide on something to find out about themselves. Because this activity takes only ten minutes, the data they use must be information they already have or can obtain easily in the class. For example, How many letters are in your name? Do you have a pet? Quickly graph the data as students say their own pieces of data, using a list, a table, or a bar graph. Then students describe what they can see in the data, generate some new questions, and, if appropriate, make predictions about what will happen the next time they collect the same data.

For full directions and variations, see p. 63.

Materials

- 300 chart (3 per student)
- Crayons or markers
- Calculators (1 per student)
- Interlocking cubes (50–60 per student)
- Stick-on notes or index cards (50–60 per student)
- Tape or glue sticks
- Adding machine tape (1 roll) or strips of oak tag
- Student Sheet 2 (1 per student, homework)

Skip Counting by Two-Digit Numbers

Introduce skip counting by finding multiples of double-digit numbers.

Just as we can skip count by 3's, 5's, or 6's and find the multiples of those numbers, we can also skip count by larger numbers like 20's, 25's, 30's, and 40's and find the multiples of those numbers. You can use tools like cubes, a 300 chart, or calculators to help you skip count by big numbers.

Note: This would be an appropriate time to review/remind/discuss with students factors and multiples of numbers. See the **Teacher Note**, Introducing Mathematical Vocabulary, in the earlier unit *Arrays and Shares* (p. 6).

Tell students that their task is to make a list of all the multiples of 30. Have students generate the first three or four multiples of 30 (30, 60, 90, 120) and list them on the chalkboard. Students work in pairs to add to the list. Make available cubes, calculators, and 300 charts.

Reporting on the Multiples of 30   After five minutes, bring the class together to report on how they found multiples of 30. Students may have a variety of strategies and ways for using each tool. For example, some students working with a calculator might use "30 + = = = = =" as a way of skip counting by 30's; other students might enter "+ 30" after every total. Encourage as many students to share different strategies as time permits.

List the multiples of 30 (30, 60, 90, 120, . . .) on the board or overhead by having students count around the class by 30's. Ask students about the patterns they notice in the multiples of 30.

Are there any patterns you see that could help us predict what number would come next? How can you check it on the calculator or with the cubes?

If no one mentions that the multiples of 30 are related to the multiples of 3, bring this up with your students.

Activity

Making a Multiple Tower

Tell students that the class is going to build a Multiple Tower as tall as the teacher using the multiples of 30 listed on the board or overhead during the previous activity. As students call out the multiples of 30 in order, one student writes each multiple in large print on either a stick-on note or an index card while another student builds the tower by taping the note or card to the wall, starting from the floor.

At various points, stop and stand alongside the tower. Ask students to make predictions about the height of the tower and the multiple that corresponds to that height.

What number do you estimate we'll land on when the tower is up to my waist? My shoulders? My head?

Encourage students to look for patterns in the list of multiples as a way of predicting what number will come next. See the **Dialogue Box**, Building a Multiple Tower (p. 15), for examples of student predictions.

Continue building the tower until it is as tall as you. Then ask students to determine the number of multiples in the tower. Discuss different strategies students use to find this number. (See the **Dialogue Box** on p. 15.)

Teacher Checkpoint

Multiple Towers and Working on Difficult Pairs

For the remainder of this session and the next, students will build Multiple Towers and practice some of their difficult multiplication pairs.

Today and tomorrow, you and a partner will be working on two activities. At some point you should choose four or five multiplication pairs from your "working on" list and see if you and your partner can help each other with strategies for learning these difficult pairs.

Suggest to students that they use the arrays for these difficult pairs. They can try skip counting the rows of squares or breaking an array into two smaller arrays ($9 \times 7 = 9 \times 3 + 9 \times 4$). You might suggest that they play some of the array games, such as Big Array/Small Array or Count and Compare, from the unit *Arrays and Shares* as a way of practicing difficult combinations.

You and your partner will also have a chance to build some Multiple Towers that are as tall as you are. Choose a number to skip count by from the following list of numbers: 15, 18, 20, 24, 32, 36, 40, 45, 55, 60, 64, 70, 72, 75, or 82. Begin to make a list of multiples for that number. Once you have 10 to 12 multiples on your list, you can begin to make your tower. You can use a 300 chart, calculators, or cubes as tools for beginning your list.

You might want to designate a particular space in the classroom for students to build their Multiple Towers. Also, since stick-on notes tend to lose their adhesiveness after a day or two, suggest to students that they build their towers on long strips of adding machine paper or strips of oak tag and then glue or tape their stick-on notes to the papers. In this way, Multiple Towers can be displayed around the room and referred to throughout the remainder of this unit.

During this session, circulate among the groups and observe students as they are involved in an activity. These are some of the things you might observe:

■ How are the students using tools such as calculators, cubes, and 300 charts to help them skip count by larger numbers?

■ Are students recognizing and using number patterns to build their Multiple Towers?

■ What strategies are students using to practice difficult multiplication combinations?

Students may need and want more opportunities to practice difficult pairs, play array games, and work on Multiple Towers. You might assign these for homework or suggest students work on them during free time throughout the day.

 **Homework**

Making Multiple Towers   Students choose two new numbers to skip count by from the following list of numbers: 15, 18, 20, 24, 32, 36, 40, 45, 55, 60, 64, 70, 72, 75. They make a list of the multiples of that number on Student Sheet 2, Making Multiple Towers. They can begin work on their new towers in school once they have finished their first tower. Students may use a copy of the 300 chart as a tool to begin their list.

Extension

Comparing Numbers in Multiple Towers   Students make towers with numbers that are multiples of one another and then compare numbers that are at the same height in the different towers. For example, if 390 is at the top of the bookcase in the 30's tower, what number will be at the top of the bookcase in the 15's tower? in the 10's? in the 3's? in the 60's?

Building a Multiple Tower

The students in this fourth-grade class are building a tower as tall as their teacher using the multiples of 25. As students call out the multiples, one student lists them on the board and another writes them on stick-on notes and tapes them to the wall. The tower is about knee-high.

Right now we are at 250, and the tower is up to my knee. What number do you estimate we'll land on when the tower is as tall as I am? Write your estimate on a slip of paper.

Kim: I think maybe 554.

Read out the multiples we have so far.

Shiro: 25, 50, 75, 100, 125, 150, 175, 200, 225, 250

Does 554 fit the pattern?

Joey: No, because the numbers end in either 0 or 5. So I don't think it could be 554.

Vanessa: But it could be 550 or 675.

David: If you look at these numbers [*referring to the ten's place*], first you add 3, then 2, then 3, then 2. See: 25, 50, 75, 100.

Let's think about which estimates are possibilities and which ones don't fit the pattern.

The students recheck their estimates using the patterns as a guide. Some decide to alter their estimates, and the tower building continues until it reaches the teacher's height at 1075.

So, we skip counted by 25's, and I am 1075. Can you figure out how many multiples are in my tower?

[*The teacher writes ___ × 25 = 1075 on the board.*]

Marci: Let's see: It's four 25's to 100, so that's 40 to 1,000, plus 3 more for 75, that's 43, forty-three 25's!

Nhat: I did it on the calculator and got 43, too.

Luisa: I broke it into 1000, then 75. Then I said how many times does 25 go into 1000. I went back to 100, which is 4, and since there are ten 100's in 1000, that's 40. Then 3 more for the 75 and you get 43.

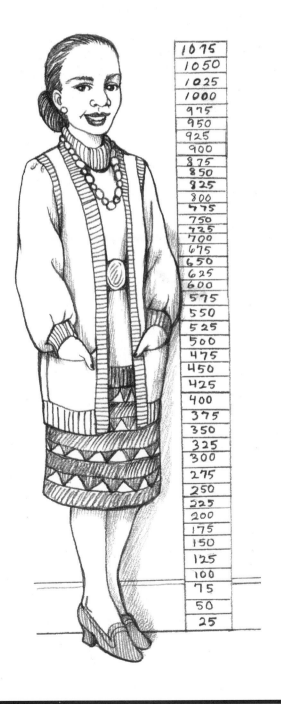

INVESTIGATION 2

Double-Digit Multiplication

What Happens

Session 1: Multiplying Two-Digit Numbers
Students are reintroduced to multiplication cluster problems. As a class, they discuss and solve a cluster problem. They also generate a set of problems that could be clustered to help them solve a double-digit multiplication problem.

Sessions 2 and 3: Solving and Creating Cluster Problems
Students discuss strategies for making close estimates for multiplication problems. They solve a double-digit multiplication problem in two different ways. Students then spend time solving cluster problems and writing cluster problems for two-digit by two-digit multiplication problems. They continue to work on difficult multiplication combinations and finish their Multiple Towers.

Mathematical Emphasis

- Using familiar landmark numbers to solve problems (for example, determining whether the solution is greater than 100, 200, 300, and so on)

- Partitioning large numbers to multiply them more easily (for example, 24×8 is thought of as $20 \times 8 + 4 \times 8$)

- Solving double-digit multiplication problems (for example, 32×21)

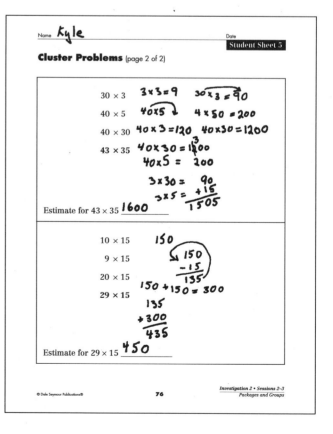

Name _Lesley Ann_   Date

Student Sheet 5

Cluster Problems (page 1 of 2)

Make an estimate for the last problem in each cluster.
Then solve the problems in the clusters.

$6 \times 20 =$ $6 \times 2 = 12$
$3 \times 20 =$ 60 $3 \times 2 = 6$
30×20 $3 \times 20 = 60$ $30 \times 20 = 600$
36×20
$30 \times 20 = 600$
$6 \times 20 = 120$
720

Estimate for 36×20 _650_

$6 \times 3 = 18$
$20 \times 3 = +60$
$26 \times 3 = 78$
26×30 780

Estimate for 26×30 _720_

© Dale Seymour Publications®   75   *Investigation 2 • Sessions 2–3*
Packages and Groups

Name _Kyle_   Date

Student Sheet 5

Cluster Problems (page 2 of 2)

30×3 $3 \times 3 = 9$ $30 \times 3 = 90$
40×5 40×5 $4 \times 50 = 200$
40×30 $40 \times 3 = 120$ $40 \times 30 = 1200$
43×35 $40 \times 30 = 1200$
$40 \times 5 = 200$
$3 \times 30 = 90$
$3 \times 5 = +15$
1505

Estimate for 43×35 _1600_

10×15 150
9×15 150
                -15
20×15 135
29×15 $150 + 150 = 300$
135
$+300$
435

Estimate for 29×15 _450_

© Dale Seymour Publications®   76   *Investigation 2 • Sessions 2–3*
Packages and Groups

16 ■ *Investigation 2: Double-Digit Multiplication*

What to Plan Ahead of Time

Materials

- Calculators: 1 per student (available for all sessions)
- Interlocking cubes: at least 50–60 per student (Sessions 1–3)
- Overhead projector (Sessions 1–3, optional)
- Blank transparencies for demonstrating strategies for solving multiplication problems (Sessions 1–3)
- Stick-on notes: 3–5 per student (Sessions 2–3)

Other Preparation

- Duplicate student sheets and teaching resources, located at the end of this unit, in the following quantities. If you have Student Activity Booklets, no copying is needed.

For Session 1

Student Sheet 3, A Cluster of Problems (p. 73): 1 per student (homework)

For Sessions 2–3

Student Sheet 4, 32 × 21 (p. 74): 1 per student

Student Sheet 5, Cluster Problems (p. 75): 1 per student

Student Sheet 6, Making Cluster Problems (p. 77): 1 per student

Student Sheet 7, Cluster Problems (p. 79): 1 per student (homework)

Student Sheet 8, Other People's Strategies (p. 80): 1 per student (homework)

Session 1

Multiplying Two-Digit Numbers

Materials

- Interlocking cubes (50–60 per student)
- Overhead projector (optional)
- Student Sheet 3 (1 per student, homework)

What Happens

Students are reintroduced to multiplication cluster problems. As a class, they discuss and solve a cluster problem. They also generate a set of problems that could be clustered to help them solve a double-digit multiplication problem. Their work focuses on:

- solving multiplication problems
- using familiar multiplication combinations to solve unfamiliar problems

Ten-Minute Math: Exploring Data Once or twice in the next few days, do Exploring Data. This activity does not need to happen in math class but during any free ten minutes during the day.

You or the students decide on something to find out about themselves. Because this activity takes only ten minutes, the data they use must be information they already have or can observe easily in the class. Once the question is decided on, you quickly graph the data as students say their own piece of data, using a line plot, a list, a table, or a bar graph. Then students describe what they can see in the data, generate some new questions, and, if appropriate, make predictions about what will happen the next time they collect the same data.

Activity

Returning to Multiplication Clusters

Put the following cluster on the board or overhead. Reintroduce cluster problems reminding students that they are a set of related multiplication problems and that they should find problems in the cluster that help them solve the last problem in the cluster. See the **Teacher Note**, About Cluster Problems (p. 21).

2×8

4×8

10×8

40×8

42×8

Students talk with people near them about how to solve these cluster problems. As they discuss and solve each problem, encourage students to think about which multiplication pairs they "just knew" and for which pairs they applied a strategy (such as skip counting or relating it to another known pair) in order to figure out the solution.

❖ **Tip for the Linguistically Diverse Classroom** Tell students with limited English proficiency to put a heart next to problems in the cluster they already know "by heart." Encourage them to show their thinking for other parts of the cluster problem by using just numbers and symbols in parentheses. For example:

$$♥ \quad 3 \times 20 = 60$$
$$26 \times \quad 3 = (20 \times 3) + (6 \times 3)$$

Note: We have not provided a student sheet for the clusters of problems students will be doing in this session. Instead, students should copy these problems on pieces of paper that can be put into their math folders or collected for your information.

When they have finished, bring the group together and ask students to focus on the problem 42×8 and explain how the problems in the cluster are related to it.

Take a look at the problem 42×8. Which of the problems in this cluster helped you figure out the solution to this problem? Were there other problems that were not included in this cluster that might have helped you with the solution to 42×8?

For an example of a classroom dialogue about cluster problems see the **Dialogue Box**, Solving 42×8 (p. 22).

Put another cluster of problems on the board or overhead:

$$3 \times 7$$
$$5 \times 7$$
$$10 \times 7$$
$$50 \times 7$$
$$53 \times 7$$

This time ask students to work individually to solve this set of cluster problems. In addition to solving each problem, students should write about how they found each solution. Remind them of the discussion that just occurred about the problem 42×8. Suggest to students that they think about which problems helped them solve 53×7. See the **Teacher Note**, Writing About

Cluster Problems (p. 23), for examples of student work on a variety of cluster sets.

Collect these papers so you can get a sense about how students are thinking about cluster problems and single-digit by double-digit multiplication.

Activity

Making a Cluster of Problems

Put the multiplication problem 74×6 on the board or overhead and ask students to think about how they might make up a cluster of problems to help them solve it.

As students suggest problems, record them on the board or overhead and ask students to explain their reasoning about how the problem they suggested might help them solve 74×6.

Students will probably have a variety of suggestions about what problems might help them solve 74×6. Once a number of suggestions have been listed, students work with a partner to create a cluster of problems they can use to solve 74×6. If there is time, ask pairs of students to post their clusters around the classroom, or students can write their clusters on blank transparencies to share them with the class.

Session 1 Follow-Up

 **Homework**

A Cluster of Problems Students make up a cluster of problems for 34×9. They solve the problems in their cluster and write about how they solved them on Student Sheet 3, A Cluster of Problems.

About Cluster Problems

Cluster problems are sets of problems that help students think about using what they know to solve harder problems. For example, what do you know that would help you solve 12×3? If you know that $3 \times 3 = 9$, you might double that solution to get the solution to 6×3. Now that you know that 6×3 is 18, you can double that to get 12×3, or you might start with 10×3. If you know that $10 \times 3 = 30$, then you can start with 30 and add two more 3's to get 36. As students work with clusters, they learn to think about all the number relationships they know that might help them solve the problem they are working on.

The cluster problems used in this unit are designed to help students make sense of multiplying two-digit numbers. They build an understanding of the process by pulling apart multiplication problems into manageable sub-problems, solving each of the smaller problems, then putting the parts back together. This process is based on an important characteristic of multiplication called the *distributive property*. You may have learned the name of this property in your own schooling without ever quite understanding what it is. In this unit, we don't teach students the name of the property, but it *is* a core idea of the unit. Here is an example: 9×23 can be thought of as $(9 \times 10) + (9 \times 10) + (9 \times 3)$. In this example, 23 is pulled apart into $10 + 10 + 3$, and *each part* must be multiplied by 9 in order to give the solution to 9×23. The number that we split up doesn't have to be split up into 10's and 1's. For instance, 8×12 could be taken apart into $(4 \times 12) + (4 \times 12)$ or into $(8 \times 6) + (8 \times 6)$. In each case, one of the numbers is split up into parts, and each part must be multiplied by the other number in order to maintain equivalence to the original expression: $8 \times 12 = (4 \times 12) + (4 \times 12)$ or $8 \times 12 = (8 \times 6) + (8 \times 6)$.

As students move into clusters that involve multiplying a two-digit number by another two-digit number in this unit, keeping track of multiplying all the parts becomes more difficult. In a problem such as 26×34, some students may think

that 34×26 can be broken into two subproblems, 20×30 and 6×4. They have not multiplied all parts of the 26 by all parts of the 34. Looking at an array for 34×26, you can see that there are several ways of breaking this multiplication problem into parts, in order to make sure all parts of one number are multiplied by all parts of the other:

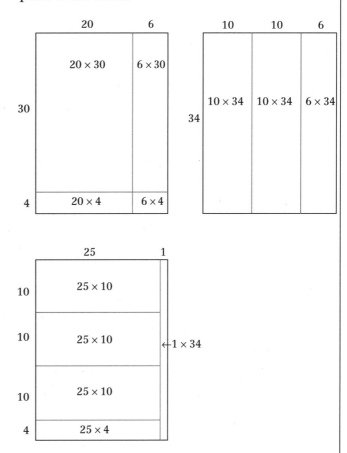

Cluster problems are intended to help students learn how to look at a problem and build a strategy to solve it based on the number relationships they know. Students work on clusters of problems that are provided for them and also create their own clusters of problems. Throughout their work on cluster problems in this unit, encourage students to add to the clusters any problems they think of that they use to solve the final problem in the cluster.

Solving 42 × 8

In the activity Returning to Multiplication Clusters (p. 18), the class has been discussing the following cluster problem in pairs.

2 × 8
4 × 8
10 × 8
40 × 8
42 × 8

They are discussing which problems in the cluster helped them solve 42 × 8.

Alex: You could say all the problems can help you solve 42 × 8 because, well, if you didn't know that 40 × 8 was 320, then maybe if you figured out 4 × 8 is 32, you would know that 40 × 8 is like multiplying by 10, so it's 320.

Rashaida: There were two problems that helped me: 40 × 8 and 2 × 8, because 42 is 40 + 2, and you multiply both of these by 8.

Jesse: Well, I kind of used those problems, but not really, because I think that 42 × 10 would have been a helpful problem. That's 420, then you just take away 2 groups of 42; so you take away 80, then 4 more.

Lesley Ann: The 10 × 8 helps because the ten's tables are easy—that's 80. Then you think of four 80's: 8 + 8 is equal to 16, 16 + 16 is equal to 32, the doubles are easy. But it's really 320, because you're adding 80's not 8's. Then just add 16. That's 320, 330 . . . 336.

Kyle: I just do what Rashaida said. You really need only two problems because you just have to think of another way to say 42 or whatever the big number is. Then you just make two problems out of it and add them together. It works every time.

So, do you think Rashaida and Kyle's strategy would work for a problem where both numbers are two-digit numbers? Let's take a look at this next problem. How might you solve it?

The teacher builds on the strategies generated by the students for solving a two-digit by one-digit multiplication problem as a way of helping them connect their strategies to a more difficult double-digit problem.

Writing About Cluster Problems

Throughout this unit, students will solve sets of related multiplication and division problems and will be asked to find and use the relationships that exist to solve the problems. When students are asked to write about how they solved a set of problems, it provides the teacher with some insights into their problem-solving strategies and how they are thinking about multiplication and division relationships. Writing about a problem often clarifies for the student a strategy that might not be totally clear to him or her.

As you observe students writing about cluster problems and as you look over their work, encourage them to be clear about how they thought through the problems and what patterns or relationships they used to help them solve the problems in the cluster. Some students may find a shorthand way to explain their thinking by using arrows or numbers or symbols. Here are a few examples of fourth graders writing about multiplication cluster problems.

$2 \times 5 = 10$
$3 \times 5 = 15$
$10 \times 5 = 50$
$30 \times 5 = 150$
$32 \times 5 = 160$

I knew the first 4, but on the last one, If I turned 32 to 30 and that is 150 then I add 2 5's and I got 160.

$5 \times 7 = 35$
$10 \times 7 = 70$
$2 \times 7 = 14$
$20 \times 7 = 140$
$25 \times 7 = 175$

I knew the first four, but on the last one I used the play money.

$3 \times 5 = 15$
$10 \times 5 = 50$
$20 \times 5 = 100$
$23 \times 5 = 115$

I know it by heart.
" " " " "
" " " " "
I did $(3 \times 5) + (20 \times 5) = 115$

$3 \times 6 = 18$
$3 \times 10 = 30$
$6 \times 10 = 60$
$3 \times 60 = 180$ $3 \times 6 = 180$
multiple
of ten so add zero

$60 \times 3 = 180$ same as above

Solving and Creating Cluster Problems

Materials

- Interlocking cubes (50–60 per student)
- Student Sheets 4–6 (1 per student)
- Student Sheet 7 (1 per student, homework)
- Stick-on notes (3–5 per student)
- Overhead projector (optional)
- Paper and pencils
- Student Sheet 8 (1 per student, homework)

What Happens

Students discuss strategies for making close estimates for multiplication problems. They solve a double-digit multiplication problem in two different ways. Students then spend time solving cluster problems and writing cluster problems for two-digit by two-digit multiplication problems. They continue to work on difficult multiplication combinations and finish their Multiple Towers. Their work focuses on:

- using familiar landmark numbers to make estimates
- partitioning numbers into smaller, more familiar numbers
- solving double-digit multiplication problems

Activity

Making Close Estimates

Put the following problem on the board or overhead:

$$56 \times 4 =$$

Many times when we have to solve problems, we can make a close estimate as a way of beginning. For example, what are some estimates for this problem? Would the answer be more than 100? More than 200? More than 300? What helps you make an estimate?

Have a few students share their estimates. Then put another problem on the board or overhead:

$$28 \times 15 =$$

Here's another problem I'd like you to make an estimate for. What are some of your ideas?

If students are having problems making estimates, you might offer them landmark numbers to think about as you did in the previous problem. Questions like "Is it more than 100? More than 500?" often help students narrow in on what the possibilities might be as well as give them a strategy for estimating using landmark numbers.

As students share their strategies for estimating, highlight those strategies where the student may have multiplied by 10—such as "I know that 28 times 10 is 280, then there are five more 25's, so that's around 400," or "Well, 20 times 10 is 200, so it's at least 200."

Distribute Student Sheet 4, 32 × 21, to students. Tell students that you would like to see how they are thinking about multiplication problems and the strategies they might use to solve them.

Explain they should solve this problem in two different ways. Remind them that in addition to finding the answer, they should communicate how they solved the problem by using equations or words.

This task is one way of assessing students' understanding of multiplication, in general, and the kinds of connections they are making among related multiplication problems. Though they have not had direct experience with two-digit by two-digit multiplication problems, they have had lots of experiences with multiplication, looking for patterns, and thinking about the structure of numbers and how they can be broken apart into manageable components. In the following sessions, students will have more opportunities to discuss and work with cluster problems involving this type of problem.

As you observe students working and as you look through this set of Student Sheets, there are a couple of questions you can focus on:

■ What types of strategies did students use to solve the problem? (repeated addition, setting up a cluster, breaking the problem into smaller problems)

■ Are students demonstrating an understanding of partitioning large numbers into more familiar parts as a way of multiplying?

❖ **Tip for the Linguistically Diverse Classroom** Have students with limited English proficiency do this assessment orally. Ask them to demonstrate how they would solve this problem by using two methods. Observe what kinds of materials they use and what kind of notation they record.

When students have finished Student Sheet 4, collect their papers. Put 32 × 21 on the board or overhead.

If we wanted to make a cluster of problems to go along with this problem, what are some multiplication problems related to this one that might help you solve this problem? You might want to think about the strategies for solving cluster problems we discussed in our last math class.

Make a list of the problems students suggest. Encourage students to explain how their problems are related to 32 × 21.

Working from the list of related problems, students work in pairs to collect a cluster of four problems they feel would help them solve 32×21. Students then solve their cluster problems.

Students record their cluster problems in large writing on sheets of paper and post them around the classroom. Set aside five to ten minutes for students to walk around and look at each other's sets of cluster problems. As students circulate around the room, encourage them to look at each cluster and see if they can understand why the authors chose that particular set of problems. They can post stick-on notes with their initials on problems they do not understand.

If you have time, have a brief discussion so students can share observations or ask questions about cluster problems they did not understand.

Doing and Writing Cluster Problems   For the remainder of Sessions 2 and 3, students work on solving sets of multiplication cluster problems on Student Sheet 5, Cluster Problems (pages 1 and 2), and writing cluster problems to go with two-digit multiplication problems on Student Sheet 6, Making Cluster Problems (pages 1 and 2). On Student Sheet 5, point out that students should first make an estimate of the last problem in the cluster before solving each problem in the cluster. Encourage them to think about landmark numbers; estimates such as "between 500 and 600" are appropriate responses.

Students can work alone or with partners. After each student makes up a set of cluster problems using Student Sheet 6, he or she can exchange the clusters with another student and solve each other's cluster problems. After they have solved them, they should exchange back and go over each other's work.

Make it clear to students that the cluster might not contain all the problems they need to solve the last problem in the group. They may need to add some problems of their own to the cluster.

❖ **Tip for the Linguistically Diverse Classroom**   For Student Sheets 5 and 6, have students with limited English proficiency continue to "write" about how they solved the cluster problems by using just numbers and symbols in parenthesis, such as a heart ♥ for problems they know "by heart."

While students are working on these cluster problems, circulate around the room and observe them working. You might also want to work with a small group of students who are having difficulty solving cluster problems.

Note: If you feel the multiplication problems are too difficult or you feel that some students are ready for harder problems, adjust the numbers according to the needs of your students.

For those students who finish early, suggest they either work on their list of difficult multiplication pairs or build a Multiple Tower for a number that has not been explored yet.

Sessions 2 and 3 Follow-Up

🏠 **Homework**

More Cluster Problems   After Session 2, assign students two sets of cluster problems (Student Sheet 7, Cluster Problems) to solve and write about. Have students exchange their cluster problem solutions with a partner during Session 3.

Other People's Strategies   After Session 3, ask students to interview adults to find out what strategies they use to multiply mentally. With the assistance of the adult, they write down the strategy on Student Sheet 8, Other People's Strategies, so they can explain it to someone else. You might collect the strategies adults have for doing one or two problems and display them on a class poster.

Multiplication and Division Choices

What Happens

Sessions 1 and 2: Division Notation and Situations   Students use a variety of division notations to represent a problem. They examine the relationship between a division equation and the situation it represents. They also discuss connections between multiplication and division. Students work in pairs on multi-step word problems that represent both multiplication and division situations.

Session 3: Looking More Closely at Division Problems   Students work on division problems by grouping or measuring out. With partners, they solve problems that involve dividing large numbers of cubes by removing groups. They discuss their strategies for using landmark numbers (multiples of ten) and keeping track of their work.

Sessions 4, 5, and 6: Choice Time   Students begin these sessions by solving a double-digit multiplication problem in two ways. They then choose from a selection of multiplication and division activities, including division problems, multiplication clusters, word problems, and Multiple Towers.

Sessions 7 and 8: What Are Numbers Divisible By?   Students find all the ways of dividing numbers into even quantities. They then look for patterns of the factors of these numbers. They discuss strategies for choosing numbers to divide by, and test their conjectures.

Session 9: Division Bingo   Students play a game that involves finding factors of large numbers. They test conjectures for finding factors and propose new ones.

Session 10: Assessing Students' Understanding of Division   Students work on an assessment task involving multiplication and division and then continue to play Division Bingo.

Mathematical Emphasis

■ Understanding how division notation can represent a variety of division situations (including sharing and grouping situations)

■ Creating a context that is representative of a division equation (for example, representing $152 \div 4 = 38$ with 152 apples divided into 38 packages of 4)

■ Using familiar landmark numbers to solve problems (for example, estimating 32×9 as 30×10, or 300)

■ Using multiplication and division relationships in order to solve problems

■ Exploring factors of large numbers (including triple-digit numbers) and developing conjectures about divisibility

■ Finding multiples

What to Plan Ahead of Time

Materials

- Calculators: 1 per student (Sessions 1–10)
- Interlocking cubes: at least 128 per pair (Sessions 1–10)
- Box or container filled with 128 cubes (Session 3)
- 20 paper cups or plates (Session 3)
- Tape or glue stick (Sessions 4–6)
- Graph paper (Sessions 1–8)
- Stick-on notes or index cards: 50–60 per pair (Sessions 4–6)
- Adding machine tape: 1 roll (Sessions 4–6)
- Chart paper: 1–2 sheets per pair (Sessions 7–8)
- Scissors: 1 per group (Session 9)
- Crayons or markers (Sessions 9–10)
- Overhead projector (Sessions 1–9)
- Blank transparencies (Sessions 3–8)

Other Preparation

- Duplicate student sheets and teaching resources, located at the end of this unit, in the following quantities. If you have Student Activity Booklets, copy only the transparencies marked with an asterisk.

For Sessions 1–2

Student Sheet 9, Pencils (p. 81): 1 per student, and 1 overhead transparency*

Student Sheet 10, More Pencil Problems (p. 82): 1 per student (homework)

For Session 3

300 chart (p. 99): 1 per pair

Student Sheet 11, Guess My Number Problems (p. 83): 1 per student (homework)

For Sessions 4–6

Student Sheet 12, 34 × 12 (p. 84): 1 per student

Student Sheet 13, Making Multiple Towers (p. 85): 1 per student

Student Sheet 14, Cluster Problems (p. 86): 1 per student

Student Sheet 15, Word Problems (p. 88): 1 per student

Student Sheet 16, Division Problems (p. 91): 1 per student

Student Sheet 17, Marvin's Mystery Multiple Tower (p. 93): 1 per student (homework)

300 chart (p. 99): 2–3 per student

For Sessions 7–8

300 chart (p. 99): 1 per student

Student Sheet 18, Finding Factors (p. 94): 1 per student (homework)

For Session 9

Completed Multiplication Table (p. 98): 5–6 per student, and 1 overhead transparency*

Student Sheet 19, How to Play Division Bingo (p. 95): 1 per student (homework)

Number Cards (p. 97): 1 deck per group of 4–5 students, and 1 deck per student for homework

For Session 10

Student Sheet 20, 287 ÷ 14 (p. 96): 1 per student

Completed Multiplication Table (p. 98): 2–3 per student

Number Cards (p. 97): 1 deck per group of 4–5 students

- Cut up a deck of Number Cards (p. 97).

Division Notation and Situations

Materials

- Interlocking cubes (50–60 per student)
- Graph paper
- Calculators
- Student Sheet 9 (1 per student)
- Transparency of Student Sheet 9
- Overhead projector
- Student Sheet 10 (1 per student, homework)

What Happens

Students use a variety of division notations to represent a problem. They examine the relationship between a division equation and the situation it represents. They also discuss connections between multiplication and division. Students work in pairs on multi-step word problems that represent both multiplication and division situations. Their work focuses on:

- recognizing division situations
- using different types of division notation
- solving division problems
- relating multiplication and division equations
- making sense of remainders

Activity

How Many 4's in 48?

48 has how many 4's?

Put the following question on the board or overhead:

> How many 4's are in 48?

Ask students to solve this problem on their own. When they finish, have them share with people sitting near them how they solved the problem.

After a couple of minutes, bring the group together and ask students to share strategies for figuring out how many 4's there are in 48.

This same problem can be written using the division sign. Does anyone know how to do that?

> How many 4's are in 48? $48 \div 4 =$

As mentioned in the **Teacher Note**, What About Notation? (p. 36), it is important for students to see division problems represented in many ways and to be able to translate the notation into a meaningful problem.

As part of your discussion, remind students that there are also other ways of recording division problems, such as:

$$^{48}/4 = 12 \qquad \frac{48}{4} = 12 \qquad 4\overline{)48}^{\,12}$$

All these can be read as "48 divided by 4 is equal to 12." Sometimes, when people see a division sentence, they think, "How many groups of 4 are in 48?" or "If I divide 48 things into 4 groups, how many groups will I get?"

Spend a few minutes reviewing with students how to read each form of notation.

Teacher Checkpoint

Connecting Division Equations to a Context

Let's take a look at the problem 48 ÷ 4. Think of a situation where you or someone might need to solve this problem. What could the situation be? What could the problem be about?

Students talk in pairs. Then ask for volunteers to share their problems that use 48 ÷ 4.

Is there a way this problem could be represented using multiplication?

Encourage students to discuss the relationship between 48 ÷ 4 = 12 and 4 × 12 = 48.

See the **Teacher Note**, The Relationship Between Multiplication and Division (p. 35).

Put a new division equation on the board or overhead. Write it in more than one way:

$$72 \div 8 = \qquad 8\overline{)72}$$

Here's a different division problem. Take a few minutes to talk with a partner about a situation where this problem might come up. Write the problem.

❖ **Tip for the Linguistically Diverse Classroom** Pair students with limited English proficiency with English-proficient students. Have the students with limited English proficiency illustrate a possible situation instead of writing about it.

As students are writing, walk around the class and get a sense of their word problems. If they are having difficulty, you might ask them what they think the division problem means. By having them interpret the equation, you can get a better sense of how they are understanding or misunderstanding the notation.

Look for examples of word problems that reflect a *sharing* situation ("There are 72 marbles being shared by a group of 8 people. How many marbles does each person get?") and problems that reflect a *grouping* situation ("There are 72 marbles being packaged into bags of 8 marbles. How many bags of marbles can be made?").

These two types of situations can be represented by the same division equation. It is not important that students be able to identify these different types of division situations, but they need to be able to recognize both contexts as situations that can be solved using division. See the **Teacher Note**, Two Kinds of Division: Sharing and Partitioning (p. 37), for more information about these two types of problems.

Have a few students share their word problems with the class. If you can, note for students which problems are sharing situations and which problems involve making groups of things. This will help students recognize that different types of situations can be represented as division problems. If there are few or none of one of the kinds, ask students to think of some.

Collect these problems and look through them as a way of assessing students' understanding.

Activity

Packages of Pencils

Introduce a real-life situation involving multiplication and division:

Lots of classroom supplies, like erasers and markers and pencils, come in packages. When I order things for the classroom, I must decide how many I need and then how many packages I should order.

Here are three problems about pencils. You can work on these problems alone or with a partner.

Pass out Student Sheet 9, Pencils, to each student. Put a copy of the problems on the overhead or board.

....

❖ **Tip for the Linguistically Diverse Classroom** To ensure the questions are comprehensible to students with limited English proficiency, read each one aloud. As you do so, show a package of pencils and pantomime an appropriate action (for example, opening the package).
....

Pencils

Pencils come in packages of 12.

1. How many packages of pencils do you have to open to give 2 pencils to everyone in our class?

2. How many packages do you have to open to give 4 pencils to everyone in our class?

3. How many packages do you have to open to give 6 pencils to everyone in our class?

Tell students they must write an equation for each problem and show how they solved it. They can use words or pictures as a way of illustrating what they did.

Some students may want to use cubes, graph paper, or calculators. These tools should be available to them.

Students work on these questions either with partners or on their own. Remind them to record their solutions using numbers in some way. Many students will use multiplication and division sentences, though some students might integrate addition into their solutions.

Observing the Students As students work on these problems, observe the following:

- What tools are students using to help them solve each problem?
- How do students keep track of steps in each problem?
- How do students use multiplication or division notation to record their work?
- Are students able to recognize a problem as a multiplication or a division situation?
- Do students deal with remainders sensibly as they answer the question?

How Many Pencils? Ten minutes before the end of this session, bring the class together for a brief discussion about the strategies they used to solve the pencil problems.

Ask students who have used different strategies or tools to share their work. Encourage them to demonstrate how they used tools to help them solve the problems. The **Dialogue Box**, How Many Pencils? (p. 40), provides some examples of student strategies and how you can help students deal with remainders when solutions do not come out exactly even.

What Did You Do with the Extras?   Depending on the number of students in your class, students might be faced with the issue of needing extra pencils and having to open a package of 12 but needing to use only a few of the pencils from the package. This is a situation where students will have to decide how to deal with the remainders. When numbers cannot be divided evenly, it is important that students address the issue of remainders in the context of the answer. See the **Teacher Note**, What Do You Do with the Remainders? (p. 39), for ways to help students accurately express remainders.

Sessions 1 and 2 Follow-Up

Homework

More Pencil Problems   Students solve the problems on Student Sheet 10, More Pencil Problems, which extends the pencil problem they worked on in class. You will need to establish with them how many people "everyone in the school" would be. You might have them record the number of people in your class and in your school on Student Sheet 10 before they take it home.

The Relationship Between Division and Multiplication

Multiplication and division are related operations: Both involve two factors and the multiple created by multiplying those two factors. For example, here is a set of linked multiplication and division relationships:

$$8 \times 3 = 24 \qquad 3 \times 8 = 24$$
$$24 \div 8 = 3 \qquad 24 \div 3 = 8$$

Mathematics educators call all of these "multiplicative" situations because they all involve the relationship of factors and multiples. Many problem situations your students will encounter can be described by either multiplication or division. For example:

> I bought a package of 24 treats for my dog. If I give her 3 treats every day, how many days will this package last?

The elements in this problem are 24 treats, 3 treats per day, and a number of days to be determined. This problem could be written in standard notation as either division or multiplication:

$$24 \div 3 = \underline{\quad} \qquad \text{or} \qquad 3 \times \underline{\quad} = 24$$

Once the problem is solved, the relationships can still be expressed as either division or multiplication:

> 24 treats divided into 3 treats per day results in 8 days ($24 \div 3 = 8$)

> 3 treats per day for 8 days is equivalent to 24 treats ($3 \times 8 = 24$)

Many elementary students are more comfortable with multiplication than with division, just as they are often more comfortable with addition than with subtraction. We want students to recognize and interpret standard division and multiplication notation. However, we do not want to insist they use one or the other to record their work when both provide good descriptions of a problem situation. In the dog-treat problem, either notation is a perfectly good description of the results.

Similarly, the order of the factors doesn't matter when describing a multiplication situation. Both examples that follow provide good descriptions of the dog-treat problem:

> 3 treats per day for 8 days is equivalent to 24 treats ($3 \times 8 = 24$)

> (3 per group in 8 groups is 24 total)

> 8 days with 3 treats per day is equivalent to 24 treats ($8 \times 3 = 24$)

> (8 groups with 3 per group is 24 total)

While some people prefer one or the other way to write these factors, we do not feel that a standard order (putting either the number of groups first or the number in each group first) should be taught or insisted on. As long as students can explain their problem and their solution and can relate the notation clearly to the problem, the order of the factors in multiplication equations is not critical.

It is important that your students learn to recognize, interpret, and use the standard forms and symbols for multiplication and division, both on paper and on the calculator. In this unit, students will use these:

$$12 \atop \underline{\times\ 3} \qquad 3 \times 12 \qquad 12 \div 3 \qquad 3\overline{)12}$$

Your challenge is to introduce these symbols in a way that allows students to interpret them meaningfully. That is, students must understand *what is being asked* in a problem that is written in standard notation. They can then devise their own way to find an answer. Notation is also useful as an efficient way to record a problem and its solution. It is not just a directive to carry out a particular procedure or a signal to forget everything you ever knew about the relationships of the numbers in the problem!

Your students may come to you already believing that when they see a problem like $3\overline{)42}$ written in the familiar division format, they must carry out the traditional long-division procedure. Instead, we want them to use everything they know about these two numbers in order to solve the problem. They might skip count by 3's out

loud or on the calculator. Or they might use reasoning based on their understanding of number relationships:

> It takes ten 3's to make 30. Then there are three more 3's to get up to 39, that's thirteen 3's so far. Then 40, 41, 42—that's one more 3—it's 14!

> Well, half of 42 is 21, and I can divide 21 into 7 groups of 3, so you double that, and it's 14.

Similarly, when students see a multiplication problem like 4×55 written vertically, they are likely to forget everything they know about these numbers and try to carry out multiplication with carrying. Instead, help students to use what they know about landmarks in the number system and other familiar number relationships. For example:

> I know that two 50's make 100, and there's four 50's, so that's 200. Then I know that four 5's is 20, so it's 220.

Students need to get used to interpreting multiplication in both horizontal and vertical form as simply indicating a multiplication situation, not a particular way to carry out the problem. So, while you help students to read standard notation and to use it to record their work, keep the emphasis on their understanding the problem context and using good number sense to solve the problem.

Two Kinds of Division: Sharing and Partitioning

There are two distinct kinds of division situations. Consider these two problems:

> I have 18 balloons for my party. After the party is over, I'm going to divide them evenly between my sister and me. How many balloons will each of us get?

> I have 18 balloons for my party. I'm going to tie them together in bunches of 2 to give to my friends. How many bunches can I make?

Each of these problems is a division situation—a quantity is broken up into equal groups. The problem and the solution for each situation can be written in standard notation as $18 \div 2 = 9$.

Although similar, these two situations are actually quite different. In the first situation, you know the number of groups—2. Your question is, "How many balloons will be in each group?" In the second situation, you know that you want 2 balloons in each group, and your question is, "How many groups will there be?" In each case you divide the balloons into equal groups, but the results of your actions look different.

> I have 18 balloons and 2 people. How many for each person?

I have 18 balloons to put in bunches of 2. How many bunches?

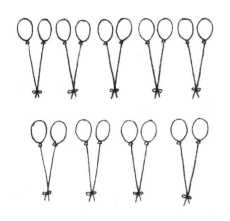

The first situation is probably the one with which your students are most comfortable, because it can be solved by dealing out; that is, the action to solve the problem might be: one for me, one for you, one for me, one for you, until all the balloons are given out. In this situation, division is used to describe *sharing*.

In the second situation, the action to solve the problem is making groups—that is, taking out a group of 2, then another group of 2, and another, and so on until no balloons are left. In this situation, division is used to describe *partitioning*.

Students need to recognize both these actions as division situations and to develop an understanding that both can be written in the same way: $18 \div 2 = 9$. Therefore, in this unit we present both kinds of division problems and, depending on the situation, help students interpret the notation as either "How many 2's are in 18?" or "Divide 18 into 2 groups; how many are in each group?"

Continued on next page

As students become more flexible with division, they will understand they can think of a sharing situation as partitioning, or a partitioning situation as sharing, in order to make it easier to solve. For example:

> How many will be on each team if I make 25 teams from 100 people?

To solve this, rather than dealing out 100 into 25 groups it is easier to think, "How many groups of 25 are in 100?"—knowing that the answer to this partitioning question will also give the answer to the sharing problem given above. Some of your students may soon have an intuitive understanding that they can divide in either way to solve a division problem.

Also, as students get more experience with both multiplication and division, they will begin to recognize how related problems can help them. Just as $2 \times 9 = 9 \times 2$, $18 \div 2 = 9$ is related to $18 \div 9 = 2$. When you find students stuck in procedures that are difficult to keep track of—such as dealing out 100 into 25 teams—ask if thinking about a similar problem might help them. "If there were 100 people in all and 25 people on a team, how many teams would there be? Does that give you any ideas about making 25 teams from 100 people?"

What Do You Do with the Remainders?

Often in division situations it is not possible to divide quantities evenly. In these cases, we have to make a decision about what to do with the remainders. Depending on the situation or context of the problem, the remainders can be expressed in a variety of ways. Consider the following contexts for the problem 36 ÷ 8 and how the remainders are expressed.

There are 36 people to occupy vans that hold 8 people. How many vans will you need?

You'll need 4 vans, with 4 people left over.

So you'll need 5 vans to take all the people.

There are 36 cookies that will be shared by 8 people. How many cookies will each person get?

Each person can get 4 cookies. Keep 4 cookies for another day.

36 ÷ 8 = 4 cookies per person with 4 extras.

or

Each person can get 4 1/2 cookies.

36 ÷ 8 = 4 1/2

There are 36 people in rows of 8. How many rows are there?

32 people fit in 4 rows. Then 4 people have to sit in row 5.

36 ÷ 8 = 4 rows with 4 more people.

or

The people fill up 4 rows and half of another row.

36 ÷ 8 = 4.5

In each of these problems, the remainder is dependent on the situation, and each answer addresses the question posed. In some situations the problem 36 ÷ 8 could be answered with just a number, $4\frac{1}{2}$. In other situations, the answer required more of an explanation in order for it to make sense ("You have 4 vans with 4 extra people, so you need 5 vans to transport all 36 people").

It is important that we teach students to consider the remainder in the context of the problem and describe the remainder in a way that makes sense to them for that problem.

A common confusion in division problems with remainders is what the remainder represents. Consider the example from the **Dialogue Box,** How Many Pencils? (p. 40), where B. J. confuses whether there is a remainder of 10 pencils or 10 people. By having students describe the remainder in the context of the problem and not just write R 10, they are solving the problem more completely and in a way that they can follow and make sense of.

How Many Pencils?

While doing the activity, Packages of Pencils (p. 32), students engaged in the following discussion.

Marci: When I figured out how many packages we would need to open so everyone could have 2 pencils, I first knew that if everyone got 1 pencil, we would need 29 pencils. So, for 2 pencils, that's 29 + 29, that's 40 . . . 50 . . . 58 pencils. So I took 58 cubes and made them into towers of 12. See, I have 4 towers of 12 and a tower of 10. So, that's 5 packages of pencils you would need.

Would you have any extra pencils?

B. J.: Two extras—but you still have to open a whole package.

Rebecca: I used the cubes, too. I gave everyone in our class 2 pencils, so I made 29 groups of 2; then I took 6 groups of 2 and said that was one package. Then 6 more because 6 × 2 is 12, and that's how many pencils are in a package. Then I kept making groups of 12. I ended up with four 12's and one 10, so I needed 5 packages.

How could you write a multiplication or division equation to show how you solved this problem?

DeShane: Well you could say 29 × 2 = 58, then 58 ÷ 12 = 5.

B. J.: Well 58 ÷ 12 is really not 5, it's really 4 with 10 extra, but you have to read the question because it says how many packages did you have to open, and 10 more people needed pencils, so you have to open another package.

So ten more people needed pencils?

Rebecca: I think you needed ten more pencils, not ten more people.

B. J.: Oh, right, pencils not people!

So if you needed ten more pencils, how many people still needed pencils?

B. J.: Five people needed pencils.

Looking More Closely at Division Problems

What Happens

Students work on division problems by grouping or measuring out. With partners, they solve problems that involve dividing large numbers of cubes by removing groups. They discuss their strategies for using landmark numbers (multiples of ten) and keeping track of their work. Their work focuses on:

- division by grouping
- using multiples of ten
- keeping track of their work

Ten-Minute Math: Guess My Number Once or twice in the next few days, do Guess My Number. This activity can be done during any free ten minutes during the day.

Choose a number for students to guess. Start by giving a series of clues about the characteristics of the number, for example:

> It is less than 50.
> It is a multiple of 7.
> One of its digits is 2 more than the other digit.

Students work in pairs to try to figure out what the number is. After students' suggested solutions are recorded on the board, they can challenge any solutions they don't agree with. When there is more than one solution that fits the clues, students ask further questions to eliminate some numbers.

> Is the number less than 40?
> Is the number a multiple of 5?

For full directions and variations, see p. 65.

Materials

- Box or container filled with 128 cubes for classroom demonstration
- Interlocking cubes (at least 50–60 per student)
- 20 paper cups or plates
- Graph paper (1 per pair)
- 300 chart (1 per pair)
- Calculators (1 per student)
- Overhead projector (optional)
- Blank transparency (optional)
- Student Sheet 11 (1 per student, homework)

Dividing by Grouping

On the board or overhead write the problem 128 ÷ 8 =. Ask students how they would interpret this problem. Then show them the box containing 128 cubes.

I have 128 cubes in this box. Some of you suggested that one way of dividing them up would be to share them by dealing out 1 cube to each of 8 people until the box was empty. Sharing is one way of doing division. Another way of dividing up these 128 cubes would be to see how many groups of 8 we can take out of the box. (If someone suggested this method, acknowledge it as his or her idea.) Does anyone have any estimates about how many groups of 8 there are in 128?

As students offer their estimates, ask them to explain how they arrived at their number. Record their estimates on the board.

Making Groups of 8 With the help of a student, begin to remove groups of 8 cubes from the box, putting them in cups or plates and lining them up so students can see them. When you have removed 10 groups of 8, pause and ask the students to figure out how many cubes have been removed from the box.

Let's see, so far we have removed 10 cups of 8 cubes from the box. Talk with the person next to you about how many cubes we have taken out and how many cubes are left in the box.

After a few minutes ask:

How many cubes have been removed from the box?

How many cubes are left in the box?

How did you figure this out?

I want to keep track of how many cubes we have removed. Many of you said that you knew 10 groups of 8 was 80, so I'm going to write 10 × 8 = 80.

Write 10 × 8 = 80 under the problem 128 ÷ 8 =.

Many of you also said there were 48 cubes left in the box. Let's see how many more groups of 8 we can get from 48.

At this point, many students might know there are 6 groups of 8 in 48. Acknowledge their thinking and suggest that you continue to pull out groups of 8 as a way of double-checking. In this way you continue the problem for those students who may not be sure that 6 × 8 = 48.

When the 48 cubes have been removed, ask a student how many groups of 8 were removed and record this on the board:

$$128 \div 8 =$$

$$10 \times 8 = 80$$

$$6 \times 8 = 48$$

Count the total number of groups of 8 removed from the box of 128 and record the answer to the problem $128 \div 8 = 16$.

Present a new problem to your students for them to solve with a partner.

Record the new problem on the board or overhead: $212 \div 4 =$

Suppose you had 212 cubes in a box and wanted to see how many groups of 4 cubes you could take out of the box. (If you assembled 212 cubes in a different container, show them to the students.) Work with a partner and figure out how many groups of 4 that would be. When we did the last problem together, I had a way of keeping track of what we were doing. You and your partner should also have some way of keeping track of this problem.

Make available any tools students might need to help them solve this problem (cubes, 300 charts, graph paper, paper and pencil). Remind students to double-check their work.

Some ways students may solve $212 \div 4 =$ are shown here.

Another Problem with Cubes

300 Chart

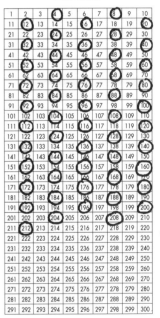

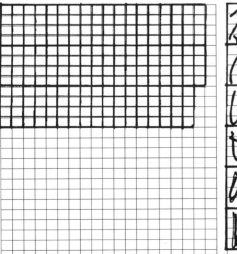

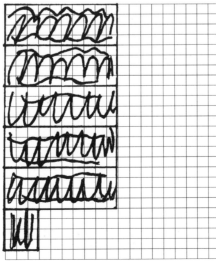

Tally

HH HH HH HH HH
HH HH HH HH HH III

$$212 \div 4$$

$$100 \div 4 = 25$$

$$100 \div 4 = 25$$

$$\underline{12 \div 4 = \quad \underline{3}}$$

$$212 \qquad 53$$

Observing the Students As students are working on this problem, circulate around to different groups and observe the following:

- Are students using cubes? If so how are they using them? Are they making individual groups of 4, or are they pulling out larger groups, such as 40?

- How are students keeping track of their work?

- Are students breaking apart the problem into more familiar problems such as $200 \div 4$ and $12 \div 4$?

- Are they using their knowledge about number relationships—for example, that there are twenty-five 4's in 100 or ten 4's in 40?

- Are they double-checking their work?

Students will vary in their approaches to this problem. While we do want students to use important landmarks and break apart problems, it is most important that students be able to understand what the problem means. Most likely there will be students in your class who will be counting out groups of 4 as a way of solving the problem. Encourage them to start using larger clumps: How many 4's are in 20? In 40? In 100? However, make sure students can really explain what they are doing meaningfully rather than simply copy a strategy you or other students use. See the **Teacher Note**, Different Ways to Do Division (p. 45), for further discussion about division strategies to encourage with your students.

Sharing Results As pairs of students finish, they can share their strategy with another pair. When most students have completed the task, bring the group members together to share their strategies. Ask pairs of students who used different approaches to share their work and to show how they kept track of their work.

At the end of this session, tell students that during the next three math classes they will be working on similar types of division problems as well as doing more multiplication clusters, building Multiple Towers, and solving problems like the pencil problem they did yesterday.

Session 3 Follow-Up

Homework

Guess My Number Problems Students solve the problems on Student Sheet 11, Guess My Number Problems. They write about why they think there is only one possible solution, or if they think there is more than one answer, they write about why they think they have all the possibilities.

Different Ways to Do Division

Most mathematics educators today do not believe we should be teaching the long division algorithm in our schools. While this may seem surprising to those of us who spent years of our lives learning to use and then teaching our students to use this algorithm, we concur with much of the mathematics education community that the long division algorithm is cumbersome and difficult and often does not lead to understanding and meaningful use of the division process.

Because the long division algorithm breaks up the numbers used into individual digits and involves many steps that don't seem like they have anything to do with division, students frequently lose their way in the algorithm. Even if they do it correctly, they probably do not think about the meaning of the numbers, what is being divided by what and why, and whether their solution is a reasonable one. Many years ago, one of the authors of this unit was working with a group of sixth graders struggling with long division. Trying to get them to really think about the division process was very difficult at this point in their school career. They were too used to memorizing a procedure and not thinking about the quantities involved. "Can't you just tell me," one of the girls wailed, "whether I'm s'posed to subtract or bring down?"

These students were trying to master procedures and steps that no longer had anything to do with mathematics. (Note that "bring down" is not a mathematical process!) By sixth grade, it is very difficult to get students to bring meaning to what they do with numbers if they have not already had significant experience thinking about mathematics in a meaningful way. It is critical that in the earlier elementary grades, we require students to develop their own approaches, based on what they know about relationships in the number system, so they become fluent with approaches to problems that have their foundation in sound number sense.

For division problems, such as those in this unit, we want to encourage students to develop strategies they can rely on that are both efficient and accurate. Consider the following problem:

I want to transport 312 people in vans. Each van can hold 24. How many vans will I need?

First, students should get into the habit of estimating the result before every problem they do, so they can judge the reasonableness of their results. For example, a student might think: "Twenty-four is close to 25. I know there are four 25's in every 100, so there would be four, eight, twelve 25's in 300, so it's about 12 vans."

Once students have made an estimate, they use strategies based on number relationships they know as well as what they understand about division. Here are some common strategies.

Successive Subtraction "Keep subtracting 24 from 312 until you can't take out any more 24's." This strategy is a reasonable beginning strategy, although even if you subtract on a calculator, it's easy to make a mistake during the many steps of subtraction required.

Making Groups "I added up 24's until I got to 96. Four 24's makes 96, which is almost 100. So I can take 96 out of each of the hundreds in 300. That gives me four 24's in each 100, so that's twelve 24's so far. Now I've got 4 left over from each 100, that's 12 and 12 more from the 12 part of the 312, so that's one more 24. So it's thirteen 24's." This approach is an important improvement in efficiency from successive subtraction. Depending on the numbers in the problem, it can be a very good strategy, as long as the student is careful to keep track of what parts of the number have been accounted for and what parts are left.

Using Multiples of Ten "I know that 10 groups of 24 would be 240. Two more groups of 24 is 47, so now I'm up to 288, and that's 12 groups of 24 so far. Then it's 12 up to 300 from 288, and 12 more to 312, so that's one more 24. So I had 10 + 2 + 1, or thirteen 24's." Multiplying by 10's is an especially good way to make groups in our number system. As students solve cluster problems in this unit, they will focus on multiplying by 10's and multiples of 10.

Choice Time

Materials

- Student Sheets 12–16 (1 per student)
- Student Sheet 17 (1 per student, homework)
- Stick-on notes or index cards (50–60 per pair)
- Adding machine tape or long strips of paper (one 5 feet long per pair)
- Tape or glue sticks
- Graph paper (1–2 sheets per student)
- Calculators (1 per student)
- Interlocking cubes (50–60 per student)
- 300 chart (2–3 per student)
- Overhead projector (optional)
- Blank transparency (optional)

What Happens

Students begin these sessions by solving a double-digit multiplication problem in two ways. They then choose from a selection of multiplication and division activities, including division problems, multiplication clusters, word problems, and Multiple Towers. Their work focuses on:

- finding multiples of larger numbers
- recognizing and using patterns of multiples of numbers
- solving multiplication and division problems

Activity

Assessment

34×12

Pass out a copy of Student Sheet 12, 34×12, to each student. Tell students that you would like to get an idea of how they are thinking about multiplication problems they have been doing and what kinds of strategies they are using. Students should work alone on this problem. They solve it in two different ways and write about how they solved the problem.

❖ **Tip for the Linguistically Diverse Classroom** Have students with limited English proficiency do this assessment orally. Ask them to demonstrate how they would solve this problem by using two different methods. Observe what kinds of materials they use and what kind of notation they record.

Assessing Students' Understanding   As you look at student papers, there are several questions you can focus on:

- Are students keeping track of their work carefully?
- Are students becoming fluent in the basic multiplication pairs?
- Do students demonstrate an understanding of partitioning large numbers into more familiar parts as a way of multiplying?
- What types of strategies do students use to solve the problem? (repeated addition, setting up a cluster, breaking the problem into smaller problems)

In Sessions 4, 5, and 6, students continue working with double-digit multiplication problems. During these three sessions you might want to meet with those students who seem to be having difficulty with these problems or whose strategies are unclear and difficult to follow.

Choice Time

After students complete the assessment task, introduce them to choice time.

Four Choices   During Sessions 4, 5, and 6 of this investigation, students may choose from four activities going on in the classroom simultaneously. This format allows students to explore the same idea at different paces. Some students may have time to complete one activity and begin another during the same hour session. If you have done other units in the *Investigations* curriculum, students will be familiar with the Choice Time format. It is important to review the guidelines for Choice Time during this session.

How to Set Up and Monitor Choices   During these three sessions, students work largely independently on four choice activities. During these sessions you might want to work with a small group of students who are having difficulty with specific activities. Enlist the help of students in the room who understand the activities to act as "resources" or "helpers" for their peers who might have questions.

For the next three sessions offer the following choices. Post this list on the board or overhead so students can monitor their own choices.

> Choice 1: Making Multiple Towers
> Choice 2: Multiplication Clusters
> Choice 3: Word Problems
> Choice 4: Division Problems

Students will need to keep track of the choices that are available and the ones they have completed. They can make a list of the activities they do on a blank sheet of paper.

Most choice activities can be worked on anywhere in the classroom. If you set up your choices at stations, show students what they will find at each station. Otherwise, make sure they know where to get all their materials. Some teachers distribute a complete set of cluster problems, word problems, and division problems to students at the beginning of this session. Other teachers keep individual pages of these problems in a central file, and students help themselves as they are ready.

Choice 1: Making Multiple Towers: Student Sheet 13, More Multiple Towers: stick-on notes or index cards; adding machine tape or long strips of paper; tape or glue; and calculators

Choice 2: Multiplication Clusters: Student Sheet 14 (pages 1 and 2), Cluster Problems

Choice 3: Word Problems: Student Sheet 15 (pages 1, 2, and 3), Word Problems

Choice 4: Division Problems: Student Sheet 16 (pages 1 and 2), Division Problems

Calculators, interlocking cubes, graph paper, and 300 charts should be available for all activities.

Choice 1: Making Multiple Towers

Students choose a number and then build a Multiple Tower for the number that is as tall as they are. Introduce Student Sheet 13 to students as you are explaining this choice. The questions on this sheet give students opportunities to reflect on their work and extend their thinking. Have students complete Student Sheet 13 for each tower they build. Students should work on Multiple Towers in either Session 4 or the beginning of Session 5 so they are prepared for the discussion at the end of Session 5.

❖ **Tip for the Linguistically Diverse Classroom** After students have completed their towers, read or have an English-proficient student read each question aloud on Student Sheet 13. If necessary, use actions to ensure comprehension. For example, if you kept building (pantomime adding more stick-ons) until you reached the next multiple of 100 (point to the number on the sheet), how many numbers (point to all stick-ons) would be in your tower?

Note: After Session 4, assign students Student Sheet 17, Marvin's Mystery Multiple Tower, for homework.

❖ **Tip for the Linguistically Diverse Classroom** Read each question on Student Sheet 17 aloud. If necessary, use actions to ensure comprehension.

Choice 2: Multiplication Clusters

On Student Sheet 14, students first make an estimate of the last problem in the cluster before solving each problem in the cluster. Students write about how they solved the last problem, including how they used any of the other problems in the cluster to solve it. It is important to make clear to students that the problems in the cluster may start them off, but they may need to add other problems themselves in order to find a complete solution. They should complete at least two clusters by the end of Session 6.

❖ **Tip for the Linguistically Diverse Classroom** Tell students with limited English proficiency to put a heart (♥) next to problems in the cluster they already know "by heart." Encourage them to show their thinking for other parts of the cluster problems by using just numbers and symbols in parentheses.

Choice 3: Word Problems

On Student Sheet 15, students work on solving problems similar to the pencil problem they did in Session 2. They should record their work on the sheets and include how they solved the problems.

❖ **Tip for the Linguistically Diverse Classroom** To ensure the questions on Student Sheet 15 are comprehensible to students with limited English proficiency, read each one aloud. As you do so, show them a can of juice, a deck of cards, and a calendar.

Choice 4: Division Problems

Students first make an estimate, then solve each division problem on Student Sheet 16. They should record their work in such a way that someone looking at it could understand how they solved the problems. Students should complete at least three of these problems and be prepared to discuss their strategies for doing division problems by the end of Session 6.

Note: After Session 5, assign students the division problem $256 \div 16$ on Student Sheet 16, page 2, for homework.

Class Discussion: Marvin's Mystery Multiple Tower

Leave fifteen minutes before the end of Session 5 for students to discuss their solutions and strategies for completing Marvin's Mystery Multiple Tower (Student Sheet 17), which they worked on for homework. As they discuss Marvin's Multiple Tower, ask them to explain their thinking.

- What patterns did they notice?
- How did they figure out what number Marvin was counting by?
- How did they figure out how many numbers were in the tower when he got to 240?
- How did they figure out the first multiple of 100 Marvin would land on?

Class Discussion: Strategies for Solving Difficult Two-Digit Division Problems

Plan fifteen minutes at the end of Session 6 for this discussion focusing on students' sharing their strategies for solving division problems such as those on Student Sheet 16 (pages 1 and 2), Division Problems. As students share their ideas, listen for evidence that suggests they are:

- interpreting the problem correctly
- breaking the problem apart into more familiar components
- using familiar landmark numbers as a way of grouping
- using known relationships to get an estimate (for example, in the problem $360 \div 11$, students may use $360 \div 10 = 36$ or $330 \div 11$ as a place to begin)
- keeping track of their work

Put this division problem on the board or overhead: $256 \div 16 =$

Here's a division problem you have been working on during Choice Time. What are some of the ways you solved this problem?

Students share strategies for solving this problem and for keeping track.

Sessions 4, 5, and 6 Follow-Up

 **Homework**

Marvin's Mystery Multiple Tower   At the end of Session 4, assign Student Sheet 17, Marvin's Mystery Multiple Tower.

What Are Numbers Divisible By?

What Happens

Students find all the ways of dividing numbers into even quantities. They then look for patterns of the factors of these numbers. They discuss strategies for choosing numbers to divide by, and test their conjectures. Their work focuses on:

■ describing relationships between factors and multiples

■ recognizing relationships among the factors of a number

■ developing conjectures about divisibility

■ using a calculator to find factors

Ten-Minute Math: Guess My Number Once or twice in the next few days, do Guess My Number during any free ten minutes during the day, but not during mathematics class.

This time when you play Guess My Number, expand the range of numbers in your clues to include larger numbers with which your students have been working:

> It is a multiple of 50.
>
> It has 3 digits.
>
> Two of its digits are the same.
>
> It is not a multiple of 100.

Students work in pairs to try to figure out what the number is. After students' suggested solutions are recorded on the board, they can challenge any solutions they don't agree with. When there is more than one solution that fits the clues, students may ask further questions to eliminate some numbers.

For full directions and variations, see p. 65.

Materials

■ Interlocking cubes or counters (100–120 per pair)

■ Calculators

■ 300 chart (1 per student)

■ Graph paper (1 per student)

■ Chart paper (1 per pair plus extras)

■ Overhead projector (optional)

■ Blank transparency (optional)

■ Student Sheet 18 (1 per student, homework)

Activity

Marbles in a Bag

Suppose you had a large number of items and wanted to divide them evenly into groups. For example, pretend you have 144 marbles or cubes and want to divide them equally into bags that contain the same number. What size bags could you make? As you are working on this problem, figure out some way of keeping track of all the possible combinations of number of bags and number of marbles in a bag.

Number of marbles in a bag	Number of bags
144	1
72	2
48	3
36	4
24	6
18	8
16	9
12	12
9	16
8	18
6	24
4	36
3	48
2	72
1	144

❖ **Tip for the Linguistically Diverse Classroom** Show real marbles and bags as you present this problem to students.

Students work in pairs to figure out all the possible ways they could bag the marbles. They can use cubes, calculators, or pencil and paper as they solve this problem. We have deliberately not provided a student sheet for this activity. Students should think of a way to organize their work for this problem.

As you circulate around the class, take note of how students are working on this problem. Are they using tools? Do they have a system for dividing the marbles, or are they using trial and error? How are they keeping track of the numbers of marbles and bags that can be divided evenly?

Organizing the Results On the board or overhead, record on a table all the ways students find to divide up the marbles. These are the factor pairs for 144.

Activity

Looking for Relationships

Most likely your students will not come up with all the combinations shown in the chart above. Many times as solutions are being shared and organized, students will see other possible solutions emerge from the information being shared. These can then be added to the table. When all solutions have been shared, look for relationships.

Let's take a look at all the different ways 144 marbles could be divided evenly. All the numbers on this table are factors of 144. You can think of a factor in a couple of ways. If you skip counted by any of these numbers or "factors," you would land on 144. Or 144 can be divided evenly by any of these numbers. Do you notice any patterns in the factors of 144?

Many students will notice that the pairs of factors are inversely related—that is, you could have 36 marbles in 4 bags, or you could have 4 marbles in 36 bags. Some students will notice relationships among pairs of factors. For example, when you double one factor, the other factor is halved as in 72 marbles—2 bags; 36 marbles—4 bags; 18 marbles—8 bags; and 9 marbles—16 bags. Encourage students to explore this relationship further. Does it work in all situations or only with certain numbers? Begin making a list of relationships students observe. Students will refer to this list in the next few sessions.

How Did You Know What Numbers to Try?   Ask students to explain how they went about dividing up 144 into equal groups. Have them share strategies for how they found these pairs of factors. Was it purely by guessing and checking, or did they have a plan for knowing definite numbers that might work when dividing 144 evenly?

If most of your students used a guess-and-check method, you might focus them on the idea of patterns by asking them:

Is 144 an odd or even number? What do you know about how even numbers can be divided?

As students generate ideas about how numbers can be divided, add these ideas to the list of students' observations.

Using the Calculator   If some students used a calculator to solve this problem, ask them to share how they used it. If no one used a calculator to solve this problem, demonstrate how it can be used to find the factors of 144.

Write this problem on the board or overhead:

$$144 \div \underline{\quad} = \underline{\quad}$$

If I wanted to use a calculator to figure out by what numbers 144 can be evenly divided, what would I do?

Most likely students will be familiar enough with the calculator to be able to make suggestions of what you should enter. If calculators are readily available to groups of students, have them test out a few numbers along with you.

Finding Factors of Large Numbers

For the remainder of this session and the next, students work with partners to find factors of large numbers. You may continue the context of dividing marbles into bags, or you may suggest a new context to students, such as arranging chairs in a theater or making a new type of egg carton that holds lots of eggs. In any of these contexts the task is to find many different ways of evenly dividing up a group of objects. For example:

If rows in a theater contain the same number of chairs, how many rows could there be and what would be the number of chairs in each row?

In a rectangular egg carton with _____ holders, how many holders could you have along its width? Its length?

❖ **Tip for the Linguistically Diverse Classroom**   Pair students with limited English proficiency with English-proficient students to complete this activity.

Students choose numbers they want to explore from the following list:

    63   72   90   105   117   180   200   254   150   98

We have purposely limited the list so that more than one pair of students will be working on the same number.

Cubes, calculators, 300 charts, and graph paper should be available as tools for students. Remind students that part of their task is to organize their list of factors in such a way that they can look for patterns in the list of factors. Students write their results on a large piece of chart paper so they can be displayed and examined by the class. At the bottom of their paper they write one or two statements about the factors of their numbers.

❖ **Tip for the Linguistically Diverse Classroom**   Model alternate ways students with limited English proficiency can record their conjectures about factors using the fewest words. For example, to convey "If a number ends in 0 or 5, then 5 is a factor," show the following:

Number	*Factor*
1<u>0</u>, 2<u>0</u>, 3<u>0</u>, 4<u>0</u>, 5<u>0</u>, 6<u>0</u>, ...	5
<u>5</u>, 1<u>5</u>, 2<u>5</u>, 3<u>5</u>, 4<u>5</u>, 5<u>5</u>, 6<u>5</u>, ...	5

To convey "If it's odd, 2 won't work," show:

    Not 2 for 3, 5, 7, 9, 11, 13, 15, 17, 19, ...

As students are working, circulate among groups and observe their processes. Take note of students who are using a system or pattern for finding ways to divide a number evenly and keeping track of factor pairs in an organized way. As students finish working with a number, have them post their results. Those who finish early can begin work on another number.

When most students have posted their results, gather the students together to examine their findings.

❖ **Tip for the Linguistically Diverse Classroom**   As you record students' conjectures, list examples next to the conjectures to ensure comprehension by all students. For example, if a number ends in 0 or 5, 5 is a factor.

Numbers	*Factor*
5, 10, 15, 20, 25, 30, 35, ...	5

Begin this discussion by asking students what they noticed about the factors of the numbers they worked on. You might suggest they share some of the statements they wrote on their displays.

These are some types of observations that fourth graders might make:

> If a number is even, 2 is always a factor.
>
> If a number ends in 0 or 5, then 5 is a factor.
>
> If it's odd, 2 won't work.
>
> If it doesn't end in 0, 10 won't work.

As students share their observations, have other students comment on them: Do they work for other numbers? Can they think of numbers for which they do not work?

If students feel there is enough evidence to support their observations, suggest that they propose conjectures. In mathematics, a conjecture is a statement for which we have very good evidence, although it has not yet been proven as always true. (If we are *sure*—that is, if it's "proven"—then it's no longer a conjecture.) Write their conjectures on a sheet of chart paper for future reference. Students may propose conjectures you know are not always true. For example, students might suggest that "Only odd numbers have 3 as a factor." For all conjectures, ask students whether they can think of the examples that support or contradict the conjecture.

Leave the conjectures posted. Encourage students to use them as resources for dividing numbers and to continue to look for counterexamples.

Using Their Conjectures After the discussion, put a number on the board and ask students what numbers they would try if they wanted to divide this number evenly. Suggest they use the list of conjectures as a way to begin finding factors.

Sessions 7 and 8 Follow-Up

Finding Factors On Student Sheet 18, Finding Factors, students choose a new number and find the factors of that number using strategies and ideas generated in Sessions 7 and 8. They should also look for new patterns.

Which Numbers Have Many Factors? Students find which numbers smaller than 40 have 6 or more factors. They look for commonalities among numbers that have many factors and use their finding to predict which larger numbers (up to 200) have many factors. They test their predictions.

 **Homework**

 **Extension**

Division Bingo

What Happens

Students play a game that involves finding factors of large numbers. They test conjectures for finding factors and propose new ones. Their work focuses on:

■ finding factors of large numbers

Materials

■ Completed Multiplication Table (5–6 per student)

■ Transparency of Completed Multiplication Table

■ Student Sheet 19 (1 per student, homework)

■ Number Cards (1 deck per group of 4–5 students, and 1 deck per student for homework)

■ Crayons or markers

■ Calculators (1 per student)

Testing Out Conjectures

Begin today's session by discussing last night's homework. Ask students if they discovered either a new conjecture or anything about conjectures made in the previous session. Have some students write on the board conjectures with examples from their homework that either support or disprove the conjectures.

Testing Another Conjecture   Some students may have noticed that if two numbers are factors of a number, then the product of the two numbers is also a factor of that number. For the benefit of those students who did not observe this relationship, you might ask:

Did anyone have a number in his or her homework that had both 3 and 4 as factors?

Some students can consult the charts that are posted around the room. They look for numbers with both 3 and 4 as factors, as well as other common factors.

Numbers that have both 3 and 4 as factors will also have 12 as a factor. Ask students to suggest some reasons for this. If students find a number that has both 3 and 4 as factors, but not 12, suggest they test whether the number can be divided evenly by 12.

Introducing Division Bingo on the Multiplication Table

I want to teach you a new game that involves finding factors of large numbers. Earlier in the year we played a game called Multiple Bingo where the object was to color in a multiple of a particular number on the 100 chart. Today I'm going to show you a new way to play this game. It's called Division Bingo. You'll need a multiplication table, a deck of Number Cards, and a calculator if you wish. The object of this game is to try to color in five numbers in a row, but this time you color in a *factor* of the number on the upturned card.

Using a transparency of the Completed Multiplication Table, demonstrate the first round of this game on the overhead projector. (Full directions appear on Student Sheet 19.) Have a student who is sitting close by choose a card from the deck and announce the number to the class. On the board list some of the possible factors of that number. Since the numbers on the cards are large, there are many factors to choose from.

COMPLETED MULTIPLICATION TABLE

	1	2	3	4	5	6	7	8	9	10	11	12
1	1	2	3	4	5	6	7	8	9	10	11	12
2	2	4	6	8	10	12	14	16	18	20	22	24
3	3	6	9	12	15	18	21	24	27	30	33	36
4	4	8	12	16	20	24	28	32	36	40	44	48
5	5	10	15	20	25	30	35	40	45	50	55	60
6	6	12	18	24	30	36	42	48	54	60	66	72
7	7	14	21	28	35	42	49	56	63	70	77	84
8	8	16	24	32	40	48	56	64	72	80	88	96
9	9	18	27	36	45	54	63	72	81	90	99	108
10	10	20	30	40	50	60	70	80	90	100	110	120
11	11	22	33	44	55	66	77	88	99	110	121	132
12	12	24	36	48	60	72	84	96	108	120	132	144

For example, factors of 240 are 1, 2, 3, 4, 5, 6, 8, 10, 12, 15, 16, 20, 24, 30, 40, 48, 60, 80, 120, 240. Students could choose any one of these factors to color in. The object of the game is to mark 5 in a row.

Some numbers appear more than others on the multiplication table; thus placement also becomes a consideration. As the game progresses, they will begin to see the need for developing a strategy so they can color in five numbers in a row.

Continue choosing numbers from the deck and having students brainstorm factors for that number, listing them on the board.

Suggest to students they also might use as resources the lists of factors they have posted around the room. Remind them that calculators are also available as resource tools. From the list on the board, students tell you which number to color in on the multiplication table. Have students justify, if they can, why they choose a particular factor. Encourage them to use the theories they have been testing out during the last few sessions. Continue playing until you feel that students understand how to play the game. It is not necessary to complete an entire game.

Activity

Playing Division Bingo

For the remainder of this session and the next, students play Division Bingo in small groups of four or five. Each student will need a few copies of the Completed Multiplication Table. Each group will need a deck of Number Cards and some crayons or colored pencils to mark their numbers. Remind students that for each new game of Division Bingo they should use a new color or symbol to mark their boards. When students first play Division Bingo, you might want to limit the game board to the 10 by 10 multiplication tables. In that case have students draw a border around the 10 by 10 table.

Observing the Students   While students are playing, circulate among the groups and observe them as they play Bingo. Here are some things you might observe:

- How are students determining factors of larger numbers?
- Are they using tools effectively?
- Are they using the theories they have begun to develop?
- What types of strategies are students using to cover the Bingo board?

Division Bingo   Students play Division Bingo at home. They will need a few copies of the Completed Multiplication Table, a copy of the directions (Student Sheet 19), and a sheet of Number Cards to cut apart into a deck.

Homework

Assessing Students' Understanding of Division

Materials

- Student Sheet 20 (1 per student)
- Completed Multiplication Table (2–3 per student)
- Number Cards (1 deck per group of 4–5 students)
- Crayons or markers
- Calculators (1 per student)

What Happens

Students work on an assessment task involving multiplication and division and then continue to play Division Bingo. Their work focuses on:

- identifying multiplication and division situations
- using multiplication and division
- finding factors of larger numbers

Assessment

$287 \div 14$

Pass out a copy of Student Sheet 20, $287 \div 14$, to each student. Tell students that you would like to get an idea of how they are thinking about division problems they have been doing and what kinds of strategies they are using. Students should work alone on this problem. They write a situation that reflects the division problem, then solve the problem they wrote.

....

❖ **Tip for the Linguistically Diverse Classroom** Have students with limited English proficiency draw a situation that describes the problem on Student Sheet 20.

....

Assessing Students' Understanding As you look at students' papers, there are several questions you can focus on:

- What types of strategies do students use to solve the problem? (repeated addition, setting up a cluster, breaking the problem into smaller problems)

- Are students able to create a division situation that reflects the problem?
- What tools do students use to help them solve this problem?
- How do students keep track of steps in the problem?
- How do students use multiplication or division notation to record their work?
- Do students deal with remainders sensibly and within the context of the problem as they answer the question?
- What strategies do students use to solve the problem? Are students breaking apart the problem into more familiar problems, such as 200 ÷ 4 and 12 ÷ 4? Are they using their knowledge about number relationships?
- Are they double-checking their work?

Division Bingo

As students finish working on the assessment task, they can organize themselves into small groups and continue playing Division Bingo.

If there is time at the end of this session, have students share some of the contexts they chose for 287 ÷ 14.

Choosing Student Work to Save

As the unit ends, you may want to use one of the following options for creating a record of students' work on this unit:

■ Students look back through their folders or notebooks and write about what they learned in this unit, what they remember most, and what was hard or easy for them. You might have students do this work during their writing time.

■ Students select one or two pieces of their work as their best, and you also choose one or two pieces of their work to be saved. This work is saved in a portfolio for the year. You might include students' written solutions to the Assessment, 34 × 12 (Investigation 3, Sessions 4, 5, and 6), and any other assessment tasks from this unit. Students can create a separate page with brief comments describing each piece of work.

■ You may want to send a selection of work home for parents to see. Each student writes a cover letter, describing his or her work in this unit. This work should be returned if you are keeping a year-long portfolio of mathematics work for each student.

Exploring Data

Basic Activity

You or the students decide on something to observe about themselves. Because this is a Ten-Minute Math activity, the data they collect must be information they already know or can observe easily around them. Once the question is determined, quickly graph the data as students give individual answers to the question. The graph can be done as a line plot, a list, a table, or a bar graph. Then students describe what they can tell from the data, generate some new questions, and, if appropriate, make predictions about what will happen the next time they collect the same data.

Exploring Data is designed to give students many quick opportunities to collect, graph, describe, and interpret data about themselves and the world around them. Students focus on:

- describing important features of the data
- interpreting and posing questions about the data

Procedure

Step 1. Choose a question. Make sure the question involves data that students know or can observe: How many buttons are you wearing today? What month is your birthday? What is the best thing you ate yesterday? Are you wearing shoes or sneakers or sandals? How did you get to school today?

Step 2. Quickly collect and display the data. Use a list, a table, a line plot, or a bar graph. For example, a line plot for data about how many buttons students are wearing could look something like this:

```
                X
    X           X           X
    X           X           X
    X           X   X   X           X
    X           X   X   X           X
    X   X   X   X   X   X   X
    0   1   2   3   4   5   6
```
Number of Buttons

Step 3. Ask students to describe the data. What do they notice about it? For data that have a numerical order (How many buttons do you have today? How many people live in your house? How many months until your birthday?), ask questions like these:

"Are the data spread out or close together? What is the highest and lowest value? Where do most of the data seem to fall? What seems typical or usual for this class?"

For data in categories (What is your favorite book? How do you get to school? What month is your birthday?), ask questions like these:

"Which categories have a lot of data? Few data? None? Is there a way to categorize the data differently to get other information?"

Step 4. Ask students to interpret and predict. "Why do you think that the data came out this way? Does anything about the data surprise you? Do you think we'd get similar data if we collected them tomorrow? Next week? In another class? With adults?"

Step 5. List any new questions. Keep a running list of questions you can use for further data collection and analysis. You may want to ask some of these questions again.

Variations

Data from Home For homework, have students collect data that involves asking questions or making observations at home: What time do your brothers and sisters go to bed? What do you usually eat for breakfast?

Data from Another Class or Other Teachers Depending on your school situation, you may be able to assign students to collect data from other classrooms or other teachers. Students are always interested in surveying others about questions that interest them, such as this one: "When you were little, did you like school?"

Continued on next page

Categories If students take surveys about "favorites"—flavor of ice cream, breakfast cereal, book, color—or other data that fall into categories, the graphs are often flat and uninteresting. There is not much to say, for example, about a graph like this:

X			X		
X	X	X	X		
X	X	X	X	X	X
X	X	X	X	X	X
vanilla	chocolate	Rocky Road	chocolate chip	straw-berry	vanilla fudge

It is more interesting for students to group their results into more descriptive categories, so that they can see other things about the data. In this case, even though vanilla seems to be the favorite at first, another way of grouping the data shows that flavors with some chocolate in them are really the favorites.

Chocolate flavors   //// //// //

Flavors without chocolate   //// /

Guess My Number

Basic Activity

You choose a number for students to guess, and start by giving clues about the characteristics of the number. For example: It is less than 50. It is a multiple of 7. One of its digits is 2 more than the other digit.

Students work in pairs to try to identify the number. Record students' suggested solutions on the board and invite them to challenge any solutions they don't agree with. If more than one solution fits the clues, encourage students to ask more questions to narrow the field. They might ask, for example: Is the number less than 40? Is the number a multiple of 5?

Guess My Number involves students in logical reasoning as they apply the clues to choose numbers that fit and to eliminate those that don't. Students also investigate aspects of number theory as they learn to recognize and describe the characteristics of numbers and relationships among numbers. Students' work focuses on:

- systematically eliminating possibilities
- using evidence
- formulating questions to logically eliminate possible solutions
- recognizing relationships among numbers, such as which are multiples or factors of each other
- learning to use mathematical terms that describe numbers

Materials

- 100 chart (or 300 chart, when a larger range of numbers is being considered)
- Scraps of paper or numeral cards for showing solutions (optional)
- Calculators (for variation)

Procedure

Step 1. Choose a number. You may want to write it down so that you don't forget what you picked!

Step 2. Give students clues. Sometimes, you might choose clues so that only one solution is possible. Other times, you might choose clues so that several numbers could fit your class. Use clues that describe number characteristics and relationships, such as factors, multiples, the number of digits, and odd and even.

Step 3. Students work in pairs to find numbers that fit the clues. A 100 chart (or 300 chart for larger numbers) and scraps of paper or numeral cards are useful for recording numbers they think might fit. Give students just one or two minutes to find numbers they think might work.

Step 4. Record all suggested solutions. To get responses from every student, you may want to ask students to record their solutions on scraps of paper and hold them up on a given signal. Some teachers provide numeral cards that students can hold up to show their solution (for example, they might hold up a 2 and a 1 together to show 21). List on the board all solutions that students propose. Students look over all the proposed solutions and challenge any they think don't fit all the clues. They should give the reasons for their challenges.

Step 5. Invite students to ask further questions. If more than one solution fits all the clues, let students ask yes-or-no questions to try to eliminate some of the possibilities, until only one solution remains. You can erase numbers as students' questions eliminate them (be sure to ask students to tell you which numbers you should erase). Encourage students to ask questions that might eliminate more than one of the proposed solutions.

Continued on next page

Variations

New Number Characteristics During the year, vary this game to include mathematical terms that describe numbers or relationships among numbers that have come up in mathematics class. For example, include factors, multiples, doubling (tripling, halving), square numbers, prime numbers, odd and even numbers, less than and more than, as well as the number of digits in a number.

Large Numbers Begin with numbers under 100, but gradually expand the range of numbers that you include in your clues to larger numbers with which your students have been working. For example:

- It is a multiple of 50.
- It has 3 digits.
- Two of its digits are the same.
- It is not a multiple of 100.

Guess My Fraction Pick a fraction. Tell students whether it is smaller than one-half, between one-half and one, between one and two, or bound by any other familiar numbers. You might use clues like these:

- It is a multiple of one-fourth (for example, one-half, three-fourths, one whole, one and one-fourth).
- The numerator is 2 (for example, two-thirds, two-fifths).
- You can make it with pattern blocks (for example, two-thirds, five-sixths).

Don't Share Solutions Until the End As students become more practiced in formulating questions to eliminate possible solutions, you may want to skip step 4. That is, student pairs find all solutions they think are possible, but these are not shared and posted. Rather, in a whole-class discussion, students ask yes-or-no questions, but privately eliminate numbers on their own list of solutions. When students have no more questions, they volunteer their solutions and explain why they think their answer is correct.

Calculator Guess My Number Present clues that provide opportunities for computation using a calculator. For example:

- It is larger than 35×20.
- It is smaller than $1800 \div 2$.
- One of its factors is 25.
- None of its digits is 7.

Related Homework Options

Guess My Number Homework Prepare a sheet with one or two Guess My Number problems for students to work on at home. As part of their work, students should write whether they think only one number fits the clues or whether several numbers fit. If only one solution exists, how do they know it is the only number that fits the clues? If more than one solution is possible, do they think they have them all? How do they know?

Students' Secret Numbers Each student chooses a number and develops clues to present to the rest of the class. You'll probably want to have students submit their numbers and clues to you for review in advance. If the clues are too broad (for example, fifty solutions are possible) or don't work, ask the students to revise their clues. Once you approve the clues, students are in charge of presenting them, running the discussion, and answering all questions about their number during a Ten-Minute Math session.

The following activities will help ensure that this unit is comprehensible to students who are acquiring English as a second language. The suggested approach is based on *The Natural Approach: Language Acquisition in the Classroom* by Stephen D. Krashen and Tracy D. Terrell (Alemany Press, 1983). The intent is for second-language learners to acquire new vocabulary in an active, meaningful context.

Note that *acquiring* a word is different from *learning* a word. Depending on their level of proficiency, students may be able to comprehend a word on hearing it during an investigation without being able to say it. Other students may be able to use the word orally but not read or write it. The goal is to help students naturally acquire targeted vocabulary at their present level of proficiency.

We suggest using these activities just before the related investigations. The activities can also be led by English-proficient students.

Investigations 1–3

tower

1. Explain that a *tower* is a tall, tall structure. Show students several pictures of towers, or draw a tower on the chalkboard (for example, a famous tower such as the Eiffel Tower).

2. Show students a tower made of interlocking cubes. Ask students to guess how many cubes are in your tower. Have students make towers with a certain number of cubes.

extra

1. Create several situations where students cannot divide objects evenly among themselves. After students divide each item, point out how many extras remain.

   There are three extra pencils. There are four extra paper clips.

2. Continue challenging students to divide objects evenly among themselves. However, this time ask them to identify how many extra items remain.

   How many extra pieces of chalk do we have? How many extra rubber bands do we have?

Blackline Masters

Dear Family,

In mathematics, our class is resuming its work with multiplication and division in a unit called *Packages and Groups*. You may recall that we began our work with these topics earlier in the year.

One of our emphases in this unit will be on recognizing when and how it makes sense to use multiplication or division in problems: For example, if pencils come in packages of 12, how many packages of pencils would we need to open in order for everyone in our class to get 4? We'll also be focusing on solving multiplication and division problems by applying number relationships the students know. For example, to solve $242 \div 22$ (how many 22's are in 242?), students might start with a familiar relationship—$22 \times 10 = 220$. So ten 22's make 220, and one more 22 gets us to 242. So eleven 22's are equal to 242, and we've solved the problem. We will also be stressing estimating an answer before solving a problem so that students can tell that their result is reasonable. And we will encourage students to develop several ways to solve problems, including use of the calculator, so that they can use one method to double-check another. Difficult computation is increasingly done with technology, and students must learn to use calculators carefully and accurately as a tool in their lives.

While our class is continuing its study of multiplication and division, you can help in the following ways:

■ Think about when you use multiplication and division in your everyday life and enlist your child's help in solving these problems. For example, how many people are we expecting for a party? How many cookies do we need if we want to give each person 4 cookies? Or, if you're going on a 3-day trip and need to travel 950 miles, about how many miles will you need to travel each day?

■ Continue looking for items around your house that are arranged in arrays (rows and columns), such as tiles on the ceiling or floor. Talk with your child about ways of figuring out the total number.

■ Play the Division Bingo game your child brings home for homework.

■ Encourage your child to explain his or her strategies for multiplying and dividing numbers. Emphasis during this unit will be on thinking hard and reasoning carefully to solve mathematical problems. Students will be encouraged to develop more than one way to solve a problem and to use methods that are based on understanding numbers and their relationships. Some of these methods may not be the ones you learned in school, but you may recognize some of them as methods you use in your daily life. One of the most important things you can do is to show genuine interest in the ways your child solves problems, even if they are different from your own.

Thank you for your interest in your child's math program.

Sincerely,

Making a Multiplication Table

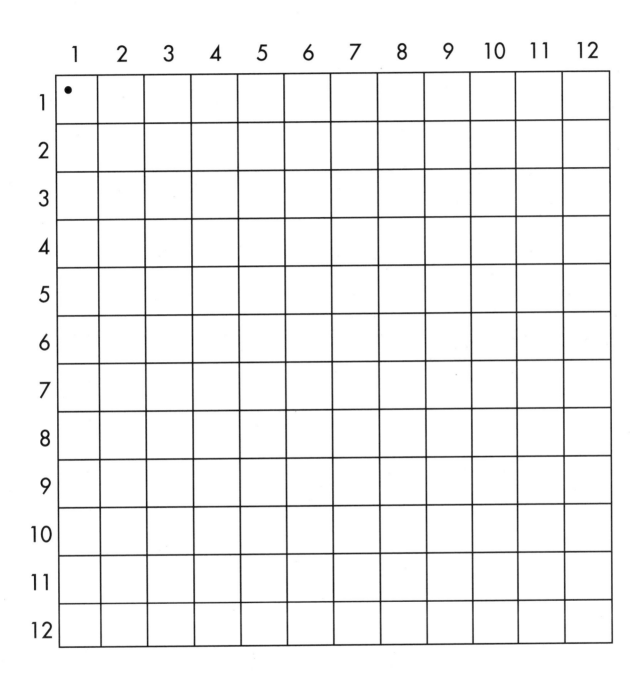

71

Making Multiple Towers

Choose any two of the following numbers to skip count by. List and record the multiples for each number.

15, 18, 20, 24, 32, 36, 40, 45, 55, 60, 64, 70, 72, 75

My first number is _____.

List of multiples:

My second number is _____.

List of multiples:

A Cluster of Problems

First, make an estimate for 34×9.

Estimate: _____

Now, make up a cluster of problems to help you solve 34×9. Solve each of the problems. Show your work and write about how each helped you solve 34×9.

32 × 21

Solve this multiplication problem in two ways:

$$32 \times 21 =$$

Write about how you solved this problem.
Be sure to include:

- ■ what materials you used to solve this problem

- ■ how you solved it

- ■ an explanation of your thinking as you solved it

First Way

Second Way

Cluster Problems (page 1 of 2)

Make an estimate for the last problem in each cluster.
Then solve the problems in the clusters.

6×20

3×20

30×20

36×20

Estimate for 36×20 _____

6×3

20×3

26×3

26×30

Estimate for 26×30 _____

Investigation 2 • Sessions 2–3
Packages and Groups

Cluster Problems (page 2 of 2)

30×3

40×5

40×30

43×35

Estimate for 43×35 _____

10×15

9×15

20×15

29×15

Estimate for 29×15 _____

Making Cluster Problems (page 1 of 2)

Make up a cluster of problems to help you solve each
multiplication problem. Exchange cluster problems
with a partner and solve each other's clusters.

$39 \times 15 =$ Estimate _____

$44 \times 28 =$ Estimate _____

Making Cluster Problems (page 2 of 2)

Make up a cluster of problems to help you solve each multiplication problem. Exchange cluster problems with a partner and solve each other's clusters.

$64 \times 31 =$ Estimate _____

$59 \times 29 =$ Estimate _____

Cluster Problems

Make an estimate for the last problem in each cluster.
Then solve the problems in the clusters.

3×25

10×25

20×25

$\mathbf{23 \times 25}$

Estimate for 23×25 _____

9×30

10×32

20×32

$\mathbf{19 \times 32}$

Estimate for 19×32 _____

Investigation 2 • Sessions 2–3
Packages and Groups

Other People's Strategies

Ask at least two family members, older siblings, or neighbors to solve one or more of the following problems mentally.

$$23 \times 9 \qquad 5 \times 32 \qquad 21 \times 14$$

With the help of each adult, record the strategy he or she used so that you can explain it to someone else. Remember to take this sheet back to class.

The problem we worked on is _____.

This was the strategy we used to solve this problem:

The problem we worked on is _____.

This was the strategy we used to solve this problem.

Pencils

Pencils come in packages of 12.

1. How many packages of pencils do you have to open to give 2 pencils to everyone in our class?

2. How many packages do you have to open to give 4 pencils to everyone in our class?

3. How many packages do you have to open to give 6 pencils to everyone in our class?

More Pencil Problems

Solve the following problems. You may use counting materials or calculators, if available. Show how you solved each problem.

1. Pencils come in packages of 12. How many packages would you have to open to give 1 pencil to everyone in our school?

2. How many would you have to open to give everyone in our school 2 pencils each?

3. If pencils came in packages of 18, how many packages would you have to open to give everyone in our class 2 pencils?

Guess My Number Problems

Solve the following problems. If you find only one number that fits, write about how you know it is the only one. If you find more than one number that fits, write about how you know you have found all of the possibilities.

1. My number is less than 50
    My number is a multiple of 6.
    The digits in my number add up to 6.

2. My number is a multiple of 75.
    My number has 3 digits.
    My number is a multiple of 100.

3. My number is less than 100.
    My number is odd.
    My number is a multiple of 7.
    The digits in my number add up to 9.

34 × 12

Solve this multiplication problem in two ways:

$$34 \times 12 =$$

Write about how you solved this problem.
Be sure to include:

- what materials you used to solve this problem

- how you solved it

- an explanation of your thinking as you solved it

First Way

Second Way

More Multiple Towers

Make a Multiple Tower and answer these questions about the tower you built:

What number did you find the multiples of?

Did your tower include 100 or any multiples of 100 (200, 300, and so on)? Which ones?

If you kept building your tower until it reached the next multiple of 100, how many numbers would be in your tower?

What patterns do you notice in your Multiple Tower?

Cluster Problems (page 1 of 2)

Make an estimate for the last problem in each cluster.
Then solve the problems in the clusters.

3×50

10×50

34×25

30×50

34×50

Estimate for 34×50 _____

60×20

62×10

62×3

62×23

Estimate for 62×23 _____

Cluster Problems (page 2 of 2)

10×43

30×40

5×43

10×36

36×43

Estimate for 36×43 _____

10×27

30×20

37×2

40×27

37×27

Estimate for 37×27 _____

Word Problems (page 1 of 3)

JUICE

Cans of juice come in cases of 24.

1. How many cases do you need to open to give one can to each of 250 students?

2. How many cases do you need to open to give one can to each of 500 students?

3. How many cases do you need to open to give one can to each student in your school?

Word Problems (page 2 of 3)

CARDS

There are 52 cards in a deck of cards.

1. How many would each person get if the cards were dealt out evenly to 2 people?

2. How many would each person get if the cards were dealt out evenly to 4 people?

3. How many would each person get if the cards were dealt out evenly to 6 people?

4. How many cards would there be in all if 6 students each had a full deck of cards?

Word Problems (page 3 of 3)

LUNAR MONTHS

A lunar month—from the day of the new moon to the day of the next new moon—is about 28 days.

1. About how many lunar months are in a year (365 days)?

2. During about how many lunar months are you in school every year?

3. About how many lunar months have gone by since you were born?

Division Problems (page 1 of 2)

Make an estimate and then solve each problem.
Keep track of your work in such a way that
someone looking at it could understand how you
solved each problem.

$198 \div 9 =$ Estimate _____

$240 \div 12 =$ Estimate _____

$350 \div 14 =$ Estimate _____

Division Problems (page 2 of 2)

Make an estimate and then solve each problem.
Keep track of your work in such a way that
someone looking at it could understand how you
solved each problem.

$256 \div 16 =$ Estimate _____

$504 \div 24 =$ Estimate _____

$360 \div 11 =$ Estimate _____

Marvin's Mystery Multiple Tower

This is the top part of Marvin's Multiple Tower.

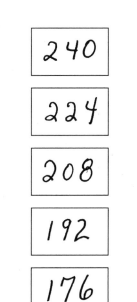

240

224

208

192

176

What number was Marvin counting by?

How many numbers are in Marvin's tower so far?
How do you know?

If Marvin added 5 more numbers to his tower,
what number would he land on?

What's the next multiple of 100 Marvin would reach?
How did you figure this out?

Finding Factors

Choose a new number. Find the factors of your
number using strategies and ideas we talked about
in class. Write about the strategies you used and
any new patterns you discovered.

My number is _____.

Its factors are _____.

Strategies I used to find the factors:

_____

_____

_____

_____

Patterns I noticed:

_____

_____

_____

_____

How to Play Division Bingo

Materials:

- Completed Multiplication Table:
  1 per game for each player

- One deck of Number Cards

- Counters (such as pennies or beans)
  to cover the numbers

Players: 1 player; a small group; or the whole class

How to Play

1. Take turns drawing a Number Card. Every player then covers one number that is a factor of the card drawn.

2. If a Wild Card is picked, the player who picked it decides on the number to be used. For strategy, the player should choose a number that helps his or her game but does not help the other players.

3. The goal is to cover five numbers in a row—either across, up and down, or diagonally—and get Bingo.

4. Players may choose to continue until the other players also get five in a row.

287 ÷ 14

Think of a situation describing the following problem:

$$287 \div 14 =$$

Write the problem and then solve it.

As you solve the problem, record each step of your work so someone looking at your work would understand your thinking.

100	180	200	60
98	32	72	150
240	144	324	225
448	396	330	450
Wild Card	Wild Card	Wild Card	Wild Card

COMPLETED MULTIPLICATION TABLE

	1	2	3	4	5	6	7	8	9	10	11	12
1	1	2	3	4	5	6	7	8	9	10	11	12
2	2	4	6	8	10	12	14	16	18	20	22	24
3	3	6	9	12	15	18	21	24	27	30	33	36
4	4	8	12	16	20	24	28	32	36	40	44	48
5	5	10	15	20	25	30	35	40	45	50	55	60
6	6	12	18	24	30	36	42	48	54	60	66	72
7	7	14	21	28	35	42	49	56	63	70	77	84
8	8	16	24	32	40	48	56	64	72	80	88	96
9	9	18	27	36	45	54	63	72	81	90	99	108
10	10	20	30	40	50	60	70	80	90	100	110	120
11	11	22	33	44	55	66	77	88	99	110	121	132
12	12	24	36	48	60	72	84	96	108	120	132	144

© Dale Seymour Publications®

1	2	3	4	5	6	7	8	9	10
11	12	13	14	15	16	17	18	19	20
21	22	23	24	25	26	27	28	29	30
31	32	33	34	35	36	37	38	39	40
41	42	43	44	45	46	47	48	49	50
51	52	53	54	55	56	57	58	59	60
61	62	63	64	65	66	67	68	69	70
71	72	73	74	75	76	77	78	79	80
81	82	83	84	85	86	87	88	89	90
91	92	93	94	95	96	97	98	99	100
101	102	103	104	105	106	107	108	109	110
111	112	113	114	115	116	117	118	119	120
121	122	123	124	125	126	127	128	129	130
131	132	133	134	135	136	137	138	139	140
141	142	143	144	145	146	147	148	149	150
151	152	153	154	155	156	157	158	159	160
161	162	163	164	165	166	167	168	169	170
171	172	173	174	175	176	177	178	179	180
181	182	183	184	185	186	187	188	189	190
191	192	193	194	195	196	197	198	199	200
201	202	203	204	205	206	207	208	209	210
211	212	213	214	215	216	217	218	219	220
221	222	223	224	225	226	227	228	229	230
231	232	233	234	235	236	237	238	239	240
241	242	243	244	245	246	247	248	249	250
251	252	253	254	255	256	257	258	259	260
261	262	263	264	265	266	267	268	269	270
271	272	273	274	275	276	277	278	279	280
281	282	283	284	285	286	287	288	289	290
291	292	293	294	295	296	297	298	299	300

Practice Pages

This optional section provides homework ideas for teachers who want or need to give more homework than is assigned to accompany the activities in this unit. The problems included here provide additional practice in learning about number relationships and in solving computation and number problems. For number units, you may want to use some of these if your students need more work in these areas or if you want to assign daily homework. For other units, you can use these problems so that students can continue to work on developing number and computation sense while they are focusing on other mathematical content in class. We recommend that you introduce activities in class before assigning related problems for homework.

101 to 200 Bingo   This game is introduced in the unit *Mathematical Thinking at Grade 4*. If your students are familiar with the game, you can simply send home the directions, game board, Tens Cards, and Numeral Cards so that students can play at home. If your students have not played the game before, introduce it in class and have students play once or twice before sending it home. You might have students do this activity two or three times for homework in this unit.

Solving Problems in Two Ways   Solving problems in two ways is emphasized throughout the *Investigations* fourth grade curriculum. Here, we provide two sheets of problems that students solve in two different ways. Problems may be addition, subtraction, multiplication, or division. Students record each way they solved the problem. We recommend you give students an opportunity to share a variety of strategies for solving problems before you assign this homework.

Story Problems   Story problems at various levels of difficulty are used throughout the *Investigations* curriculum. The two story problem sheets provided here help students review and maintain skills that have already been taught. You can also make up other problems in this format, using numbers and contexts that are appropriate for your students. Students solve the problems and then record their strategies.

Froggy Races   This type of problem is introduced in the unit *Landmarks in the Thousands*. Here, you are provided three problem sheets and one 300 chart, which you can copy for use with the problem sheets. You can also make up other problems in this format, using numbers that are appropriate for your students. On each sheet, students solve the problems and record their solution strategies.

How to Play 101 to 200 Bingo

Materials
- 101 to 200 Bingo Board
- One deck of Numeral Cards
- One deck of Tens Cards
- Colored pencil, crayon, or marker

Players: 2 or 3

How to Play

1. Each player takes a 1 from the Numeral Card deck and keeps this card throughout the game.

2. Shuffle the two decks of cards. Place each deck face down on the table.

3. Players use just one Bingo Board. You will take turns and work together to get a Bingo.

4. To determine a play, draw two Numeral Cards and one Tens Card. Arrange the 1 and the two other numerals to make a number between 100 and 199. Then add or subtract the number on your Tens Card. Circle the resulting number on the 101 to 200 Bingo Board.

5. Wild Cards in the Numeral Card deck can be used for any numeral from 0 through 9. Wild Cards in the Tens Card deck can be used as + or – any multiple of 10 from 10 through 70.

6. Some combinations cannot land on the 101 to 200 Bingo Board at all. Make up your own rules about what to do when this happens. (For example, a player could take another turn, or the Tens Card could be *either* added or subtracted in this instance.)

7. The goal is for the players together to circle five adjacent numbers in a row, in a column, or on a diagonal. Five circled numbers is a Bingo.

101	102	103	104	105	106	107	108	109	110
111	112	113	114	115	116	117	118	119	120
121	122	123	124	125	126	127	128	129	130
131	132	133	134	135	136	137	138	139	140
141	142	143	144	145	146	147	148	149	150
151	152	153	154	155	156	157	158	159	160
161	162	163	164	165	166	167	168	169	170
171	172	173	174	175	176	177	178	179	180
181	182	183	184	185	186	187	188	189	190
191	192	193	194	195	196	197	198	199	200

Practice Page
Packages and Groups

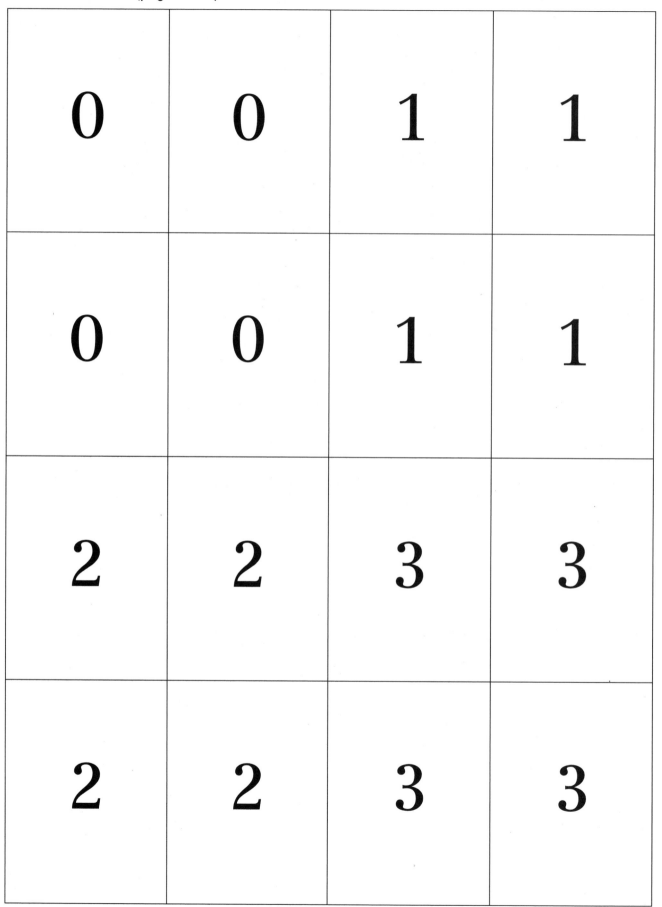

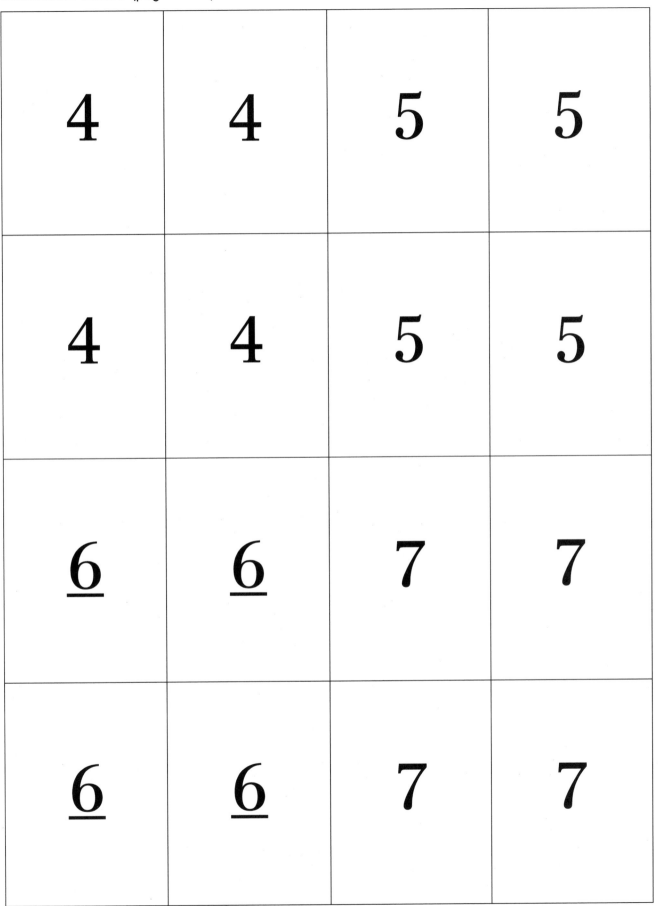

Practice Page
Packages and Groups

8	8	<u>9</u>	<u>9</u>
8	8	<u>9</u>	<u>9</u>
WILD CARD	**WILD CARD**		
WILD CARD	**WILD CARD**		

+10	**+10**	**+10**	**+10**
+20	**+20**	**+20**	**+20**
+30	**+30**	**+30**	**+40**
+40	**+50**	**+50**	**+60**
+70	**WILD CARD**	**WILD CARD**	**WILD CARD**

Practice Page
Packages and Groups

-10	**-10**	**-10**	**-10**
-20	**-20**	**-20**	**-20**
-30	**-30**	**-30**	**-40**
-40	**-50**	**-50**	**-60**
-70	**WILD CARD**	**WILD CARD**	**WILD CARD**

Practice Page A

Solve this problem in two different ways, and
write about how you solved it:

12 × 4 =

Here is the first way I solved it:

Here is the second way I solved it:

Practice Page B

Solve this problem in two different ways, and write about how you solved it:

63 ÷ 7 =

Here is the first way I solved it:

Here is the second way I solved it:

Practice Page C

For each problem, show how you found your solution.

1. Six people gathered 45 oranges from a tree. How many oranges did each one take home?

2. I have 45 oranges. I want to put them in boxes that hold 6 oranges each. How many boxes will I need?

3. I bought 6 oranges. I spent 4 dollars and 50 cents. How much did I spend on each orange?

Practice Page D

For each problem, show how you found your solution.

1. Tennis balls come in packages of three. Juan needs 245 balls for an upcoming tournament. How many packages will he have to buy?

2. Ten packages of tennis balls fit in a box. How many boxes will Juan have when he buys the 245 tennis balls he needs?

3. Juan can fit as many as 7 boxes in the trunk of his car. How many will he need to put elsewhere in his car?

1	2	3	4	5	6	7	8	9	10
11	12	13	14	15	16	17	18	19	20
21	22	23	24	25	26	27	28	29	30
31	32	33	34	35	36	37	38	39	40
41	42	43	44	45	46	47	48	49	50
51	52	53	54	55	56	57	58	59	60
61	62	63	64	65	66	67	68	69	70
71	72	73	74	75	76	77	78	79	80
81	82	83	84	85	86	87	88	89	90
91	92	93	94	95	96	97	98	99	100
101	102	103	104	105	106	107	108	109	110
111	112	113	114	115	116	117	118	119	120
121	122	123	124	125	126	127	128	129	130
131	132	133	134	135	136	137	138	139	140
141	142	143	144	145	146	147	148	149	150
151	152	153	154	155	156	157	158	159	160
161	162	163	164	165	166	167	168	169	170
171	172	173	174	175	176	177	178	179	180
181	182	183	184	185	186	187	188	189	190
191	192	193	194	195	196	197	198	199	200
201	202	203	204	205	206	207	208	209	210
211	212	213	214	215	216	217	218	219	220
221	222	223	224	225	226	227	228	229	230
231	232	233	234	235	236	237	238	239	240
241	242	243	244	245	246	247	248	249	250
251	252	253	254	255	256	257	258	259	260
261	262	263	264	265	266	267	268	269	270
271	272	273	274	275	276	277	278	279	280
281	282	283	284	285	286	287	288	289	290
291	292	293	294	295	296	297	298	299	300

Practice Page E

Solve each problem. You may want to use a 300 chart to help.

1. Two frogs had a race. Green Frog took 14 jumps of 20. Gray Frog took 8 jumps of 35. Who was ahead? How do you know?

2. In a second race, Green took 6 jumps of 45. Gray took 9 jumps of 30. Who was ahead? How do you know?

3. In the last race, Green decided to take jumps of 50. He took 3 jumps of 50. How many more jumps of 50 did he need to reach 300? How do you know?

Practice Page F

Solve each problem. You may want to use a 300 chart to help.

1. Two frogs had a race. Keeper Frog took 2 jumps of 89. Kaller Frog took 3 jumps of 60. Who was ahead? How do you know?

2. In a second race, Keeper took 4 jumps of 55. Kaller took 6 jumps of 36. Who was ahead? How do you know?

3. In the last race, Kaller decided to take jumps of 75. She took 3 jumps of 75. How many more jumps of 75 did she need to reach 300? How do you know?

Practice Page G

Solve each problem. You may want to use a 300 chart to help.

1. Two frogs had a race. Lemon Frog took 15 jumps of 8. Lime Frog took 30 jumps of 4. Who was ahead? How do you know?

2. In a second race, Lemon took 8 jumps of 18. Lime took 12 jumps of 12. Who was ahead? How do you know?

3. In the last race, Lime decided to take jumps of 25. She took 7 jumps of 25. How many more jumps of 25 did she need to reach 300? How do you know?